Gobbet
Junior High School
Library

# The Seven Wonders of the Ancient World

*Robert Silverberg*

# The Seven Wonders of the Ancient World

*Illustrations by Paul Williams*

CROWELL-COLLIER PRESS / Collier-Macmillan Limited, London

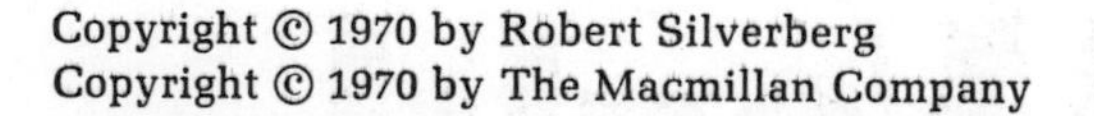



Library of Congress Catalog Card Number 70-95298

The Macmillan Company
866 Third Avenue
New York, New York 10022

Collier-Macmillan Canada Ltd., Toronto, Ontario

Printed in the United States of America

*10 9 8 7 6 5 4 3 2*

# Contents

# The Seven Wonders of the Ancient World

# The Seven Wonders

NORTH
BLACK SEA
EPHESUS
HALICARNASSUS
RHODES
SEA
ALEXANDRIA
BABYLON
GIZEH

In the middle of the second century before the birth of Christ, a poet named Antipater drew up a list of seven marvelous structures—the Seven Wonders of the World. Antipater was a Greek who lived in the city of Sidon, then a Phoenician port, now part of the country of Lebanon. His list was meant as a kind of summary of mankind's outstanding artistic accomplishments.

He was not the first to draw up such a list, nor was he the last; the Greeks were particularly fond of compiling them. Aside from Antipater's list, though, only one other nearly complete selection of the Seven Wonders has come down to us. It is the one included in a little book said to have been written by a famous Greek engineer and mathematician, Philon of Byzantium, who lived about the same time as Antipater. (Most scholars believe that Philon had nothing to do with the book that bears his name; they think it was written long after his death, and that his name was put on it by an unknown writer trying to become more widely recognized by using a well-known signature.)

Since most of those who played the game of "Seven Wonders" were Greeks, it should not be surprising that most of the wonders listed were examples of Greek culture. Actually, only two of the seven were located in present-day Greece: the Statue of Zeus at Olympia, and the Colossus of Rhodes. Of the others, three—not including the Great Pyramid of Egypt and the Hanging Gardens of Babylon—were the products of Greek artistry and Greek ingenuity, even though they happen to be found in Turkey or Egypt.

The various lists of the Seven Wonders are not quite identical. But they do agree on six out of the seven:

- The Great Pyramid of Egypt
- The Hanging Gardens of Babylon
- The Statue of Zeus at Olympia

- The Temple of Artemis at Ephesus
- The Mausoleum of Halicarnassus
- The Colossus of Rhodes

On some of the early Greek lists, seventh place is awarded to the Walls of Babylon. On other lists it goes to the Palace of Cyrus, king of Persia. However, somewhere along the way both of these were dropped, and by the sixth century A.D., when the list took its final form, the seventh wonder was given as:

- The Lighthouse of Alexandria

Those are the Seven. At no time did all seven exist simultaneously, so the many lists could not possibly have been drawn up, as is so often said, as guidebooks for ancient travelers. Most tourists of the ancient world did hope to see as many of the Seven Wonders as possible; but the Colossus of Rhodes was a pile of scrap metal by the time Antipater of Sidon was born, and the Hanging Gardens of Babylon were in ruins before the Colossus was erected. Of the Seven Wonders, only the Great Pyramid exists in reasonably intact form today; fragments of a few of the others have been found by archaeologists, and some are totally gone.

It is interesting to consider some of the wonders of the ancient world that failed to make the list. One might nominate Egypt's Sphinx, that great crouching lion with a pharoah's head, or the mighty statues of Rameses II at Abu Simbel on the Nile River. Perhaps the listmakers felt that the Great Pyramid might well serve to represent all of Egypt's splendid monuments, though. Stonehenge, that mysterious arrangement of huge stones on England's Salisbury Plain, was among the most awesome achievements of prehistoric man; but the Greeks knew nothing about it. Nor had they ever heard of the Great Wall of China, which surely deserved a place on the list of wonders. Completed in 214 B.C., the wall was a snakelike line of stone and brick and mud, running more than eighteen hundred miles along China's northern border.

Other listmakers might suggest the Temple of Solomon in Jerusalem, destroyed and rebuilt again and again over a period of a thousand years. Antipater lived only a few days' journey from Jerusalem and may have visited it, but possibly he thought it might be an insult to Zeus, Apollo, and Artemis to make them share the list with a building sacred to the god of another nation. Nor could the vast Colosseum of Rome, where gladiators clashed, go on the list; it was not begun until A.D. 72, long after the lists of wonders were compiled.

Antipater and his colleagues might also have considered placing on their lists the Palace of Minos in Crete; but that had been shattered by an earthquake more than a thousand years before their time and had been forgotten except in the myth of Theseus and the Labyrinth. They might have named the Temple of Apollo at Delphi, or the Parthenon at Athens, or any of a dozen other marvels. But none of those was chosen.

Why *seven* wonders?

There is no necessary reason why the number was fixed at seven. The lists might just as easily have been composed of five wonders, or eleven, or thirty-two. However, a list of seven is convenient: not too long to be memorized, not so short that it omits a great deal. Also, the number seven has been considered a sacred or lucky number by many cultures. The ancient astronomers believed there were seven planets; they knew nothing of Uranus, Neptune, or Pluto, but counted the moon as a planet to round out the list. The Bible is full of groupings of seven: seven days of the week, seven days of Creation, seven lean years. When

Joshua laid siege to Jericho, seven priests with seven trumpets marched around the city once every day, but seven times on the seventh day. There are seven virtues and seven deadly sins. The Greeks had a list of seven wise men, though they never could agree on which seven philosophers belonged on it. Pythagoras, the Greek mathematician of the sixth century B.C., who believed that the essence of all wisdom lay in numbers, regarded the number seven as of special mystic significance.

We still speak of the seven seas, the seven hills of Rome, the seven years of hard luck, and many more. The Seven Wonders of the Ancient World, then, fit quite naturally into these seven-sided arrangements. Let us begin our tour of them with the oldest of the seven, the largest, and the only one that remains to us—the Great Pyramid of Egypt.

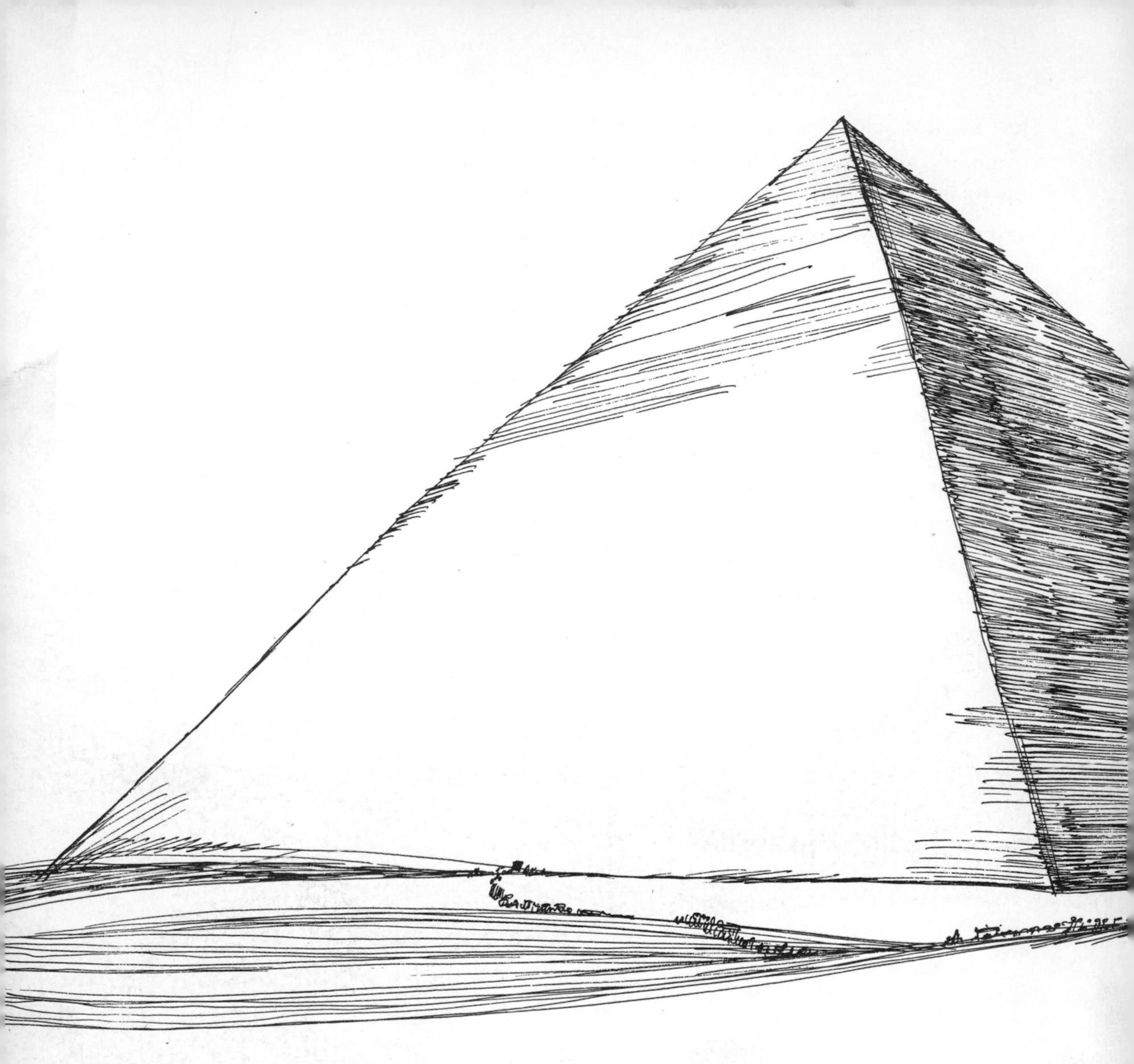

# 1. The Great Pyramid of Egypt

Perhaps the most inquisitive traveler who ever lived was Herodotus of Halicarnassus, whom the Roman writer Cicero called "the Father of History." Halicarnassus, where Herodotus was born about 484 B.C., was a Greek colony on the coast of Asia Minor. At the time of his birth the area had come under the control of the Persians, and today it is part of Turkey. When he was a young man Herodotus got into political difficulties in his native city and was obliged to go abroad, beginning an extraordinary career of seeing sights and gathering strange facts.

He lived a while in Athens, where he got to know the wise ruler Pericles, the playwright Sophocles, and other great men of that golden age of Greek civilization. He traveled through the many islands in the Aegean Sea; he visited Egypt and went far up the Nile; he journeyed down the Euphrates River to view the famed city of Babylon; he toured the Phoenician coast, seeing the lands that now make up Lebanon and Israel. Most amazingly, he ventured into the territory of Scythia, north of the Black Sea in what now is Russia—a land then occupied by barbarians and rarely entered by civilized men.

Wherever he went, Herodotus saw the important sights and probed into matters of history, culture, and folklore. He met with priests, scholars, and princes; but he also collected information from ordinary folk, from anyone who could spin an interesting tale. He particularly sought to learn things about the lands beyond the reach of his travels —India, western Europe, and Africa south of Egypt.

After seventeen years of roaming, Herodotus began to assemble his mass of material into a book, which he went on polishing and revising until his death, about 426 B.C. Supposedly the book was a history of the war between Greece and Persia—the great event of Herodotus' youth, covering more than fifty years and ending with a Greek victory in 479 B.C. But the opening lines of the work tell us that his real purpose was a much broader one: "These are the researches of Herodotus of Halicarnassus, which he publishes, in order that the memory of the past may not be blotted out from among men by time, and that great and marvelous deeds done by Greeks and foreigners, and especially the reason why they warred against each other, may not lack renown."

To explain the war between the Greeks and the Persians, Herodotus first had to explain the rise of Persian power; to do this, he had to tell of Egypt and Babylonia and all the other lands conquered by the Persians; and, as one thing led to another, he found himself writing a rambling history of most of the known world of his day. Because he could never resist telling a good story, Herodotus included delightful bits of mythology, natural history, anthropology, and pure gossip; and the result, while not altogether reliable as a work of scholarship, was one of the most entertaining works of history ever composed.

While he was in Egypt, of course, Herodotus paid a call on that country's most celebrated tourist attraction: the Pyramids at Gizeh. Egypt has many pyramids great and small—there are sixty-seven of them scattered around Cairo alone. But when one speaks of the Pyramids, one means those three gigantic piles of stone blocks that rise from the desert a few miles west of the Nile, near the village of Gizeh, and not far from Egypt's modern capital, Cairo.

The three immense structures were erected some 4500 years ago, as tombs for three kings: Khufu, Khafre, and Menkure. The Pyramids were already incredibly ancient when Herodotus came to view them; in fact, they were older in the time of Herodotus than most of the other six of the Seven Wonders would be now, if they still existed.

He was mainly interested in the oldest and largest of the Pyramids, that of Khufu, which later would be classed among the Seven Wonders of the Ancient World. Even as we can do today, Herodotus explored the Great Pyramid of Khufu in the company of professional Egyptian guides. The guides, like all members of their trade both ancient and modern, liked to make a visit to a famous place even more exciting by telling wonderful stories of its history. And in the manner of guides of every era and every land, they knew how to make up fantastic tales to fill in those places where they did not happen to know the real facts.

Herodotus, who was a trifle gullible, solemnly wove all these legends into his book. He devoted several pages to the Pyramids, using Greek forms of the names of the monarchs for whom they were built: Cheops for Khufu, Chephren for Khafre, Mycerinus for Menkure. In those few pages Herodotus managed to give immortality to a whole collection of Pyramid myths, which historians ever since have worked hard to disprove.

For example, his guides told him that when "Cheops succeeded to the throne, [he] plunged into all manner of wickedness. He closed the temples, and forbade the Egyptians to offer sacrifice, compelling them instead to labor, one and all, in his service. Some were required to drag blocks of stone down to the Nile from the quarries in the Arabian range of hills; others received the blocks after they had been conveyed in boats across the river, and drew them to the range of hills called the Libyan. A hundred thousand men labored constantly, and were relieved every three months by a fresh lot."

It took "ten years' oppression of the people," says Herodotus, simply to build the stone highway leading to the site of the Great Pyramid, the small temples about it and the underground burial chamber of the Pharaoh. Cheops' tomb, he relates, was located "on a sort of island, surrounded by water introduced from the Nile by a canal," all of it underneath the Pyramid.

"The Pyramid itself was twenty years in building," he

declares. "It is a square, eight hundred feet each way, and the height the same, built entirely of polished stone, fitted together with the utmost care. The stones of which it is composed are none of them less than thirty feet in length." The construction of the Pyramid was carried out step by step, by laying a base, a slightly smaller level of blocks on top of that, a smaller one still above that, and so on to the top. Herodotus claimed that the immense stone blocks were lifted to their places "by means of machines formed of short wooden planks. The first machine raised them from the ground to the top of the first step. On this there was another machine, which received the stone upon its arrival, and conveyed it to the second step, whence a third machine advanced it still higher."

Herodotus saw an inscription in Egyptian hieroglyphic writing on the side of the Great Pyramid. He asked his guide what it said and was told that it was a record of "the quantity of radishes, onions, and garlic consumed by the laborers who constructed it. And I perfectly well remember that the interpreter who read the writing to me said that the money expended in this way was 1600 talents of silver. [The Egyptian talent was about 56 pounds of silver—worth $1500 or so at today's price, much more then.] If this then is a true record, what a vast sum must have been spent on the iron tools used in the work, and on the feeding and clothing of the laborers, considering the length of time the work lasted. . . ."

Sorting the truth from the fantasy in Herodotus' account is a difficult matter. The hieroglyphic inscription on the Pyramid's side, for instance, vanished a long time ago, so we cannot say what it really meant. But the inscription was much more likely a declaration of praise for Khufu than a record of the "radishes, onions, and garlic" eaten by the workmen.

There is no doubt at all about the size of the Great Pyramid. There it still stands, a little battered and weather-beaten after 45 centuries, but mostly intact. At its base it measures about 756 feet in length along each of the four sides. (No two of the sides are absolutely identical in length, but the difference between the longest and the shortest is only 7.9 inches.) It rises to a height of 450 feet. Once it was 30 feet taller than that, but the Arabs who invaded Egypt about A.D. 650 stole the uppermost blocks of stone to use in the construction of their own buildings near what now is Cairo. The Great Pyramid could never have reached the height of 800 feet that Herodotus claims for it, since the angles of its base make such a height a geometric impossibility.

The bulk of the Pyramid is enormous. It is made up of 2,300,000 blocks of stone, each averaging two and a half tons in weight; the biggest blocks weigh fifteen tons. If these blocks were cut into cubes a foot high, wide, and deep, and were placed side by side along the equator, they would reach two-thirds of the way around the world. Napoleon, who visited the Pyramids in 1798 when he led an army of conquest into Egypt, calculated—correctly—that the Great Pyramid and its two smaller companions contained enough stone to build a wall ten feet high and one foot wide all the way around France. The area of the base of the Great Pyramid is so large that the cathedrals of Florence and Milan, as well as St. Peter's in Rome and St. Paul's in London, could all be placed together inside it, with enough room left for Westminster Abbey.

The Great Pyramid was extraordinary not only in size but in the quality of its workmanship. Today, the original beauty of the Pyramid is gone, and the huge structure must be viewed from a distance in order to see the simplicity and perfection of its unusual shape. At closer range one sees that the outside of the structure is a series of rough stone blocks forming a kind of immense four-sided staircase; energetic tourists used to climb those tremendous "stairs," but the Egyptian government has forbidden that now, since too many people grew dizzy and fell off.

In its present form the Great Pyramid has the raw power of hugeness, but when Herodotus saw it, it must also have been beautiful. In his time the Pyramid was covered with a casing of white limestone blocks, smooth and fine, which turned its sides into steeply sloping, perfectly flat surfaces. That must have been impressive to behold—especially when the bright Egyptian sunlight glistened on the gleaming stone. But the smooth white casing was peeled away about a thousand years ago by the Arabs, who used it in the bridges and houses of Cairo. Only a few small patches remain at the base, although the neighboring Pyramid of Khafre still has the topmost hundred feet of its casing.

The accuracy with which the limestone blocks of casing were put in place is one of the reasons why the Great Pyramid was deemed a wonder of the world. The British archaeologist William Matthews Flinders Petrie, who examined the remaining casing at the base of the Great Pyramid in 1881, found that the stone blocks had been cut so carefully that the average distance between them was only one-fiftieth of an inch, and in places they were as close as one-five hundredth of an inch. The builders then had managed to fill the microscopic space between the stones with cement.

The placing of the Great Pyramid was equally perfect. Flinders Petrie called it "a triumph of skill; its errors, both in length and in angles, could be covered by placing one's thumb on them." Though lacking any of the instruments of a modern surveyor, the architects of Khufu's Pyramid laid it out so that its four sides were almost exactly lined up with true north, south, east, and west. The variations from mathematical perfection were so slight that they can be detected only by careful calculation. Each of the Pyramid's four corners is a nearly perfect right angle, also; the greatest variation from the proper ninety-degree angle is less than *one-twentieth of a degree.* How such accuracy was achieved is a baffling puzzle; the architects must have used the sun and the stars as their guides, but it is still not easy to understand how relatively primitive surveying methods produced such startling results.

Nor—despite Herodotus—are we certain how the workmen handled the job of putting the massive stone blocks into position. Herodotus speaks of "machines formed of short wooden planks" that were used to hoist the blocks from level to level. That seems to refer to some sort of construction crane, or perhaps a kind of pulley arrangement.

But the highly pictorial murals on the walls of Egyptian tombs, which are our chief sources of information about daily life in ancient Egypt, show no such "machines." Nor is there any reference to them in Egyptian literature, and archaeologists have found no traces of them. It appears that Herodotus must have misunderstood what his guides were telling him—or perhaps he fell for another of their tall tales.

There has been much talk about the "secret" of the ancient Egyptian engineers, the supposedly lost method by which they moved the giant blocks of stone to the site of the Pyramid; but recent research has shown that the secret was quite a simple one. According to current archaeological beliefs, the Egyptians did the whole job with crowbars, ramps, sledges, rollers—and practically unlimited manpower.

The stone was quarried on the opposite side of the Nile, near Cairo. Metal saws tipped with jewels were used to cut grooves into the rock of the quarry. Holes were drilled, and wooden pegs inserted. When water was poured over the pegs, they swelled and split the rock, cracking loose huge blocks.

Workmen using crowbars tipped each giant block up on one side and maneuvered it until a wooden sledge could be slipped into place underneath it. The block was lashed to the sledge by thick ropes; then both block and sledge may have been lifted again so that round logs to serve as rollers could be placed under them. Then gangs of men would haul the sledge to the river, where the block was carefully loaded onto a great barge and floated across. On the other side, block and sledge were hauled by the same method to the site chosen for Khufu's tomb.

The pyramid-builders may not even have used rollers under the sledges. On the wall of a tomb of an Egyptian nobleman who lived about eight hundred years after the Great Pyramid was constructed, there is a painting that shows a team of workers hauling a stone statue that must have weighed at least sixty tons. It is mounted on a sledge pulled by 172 men, but there are no rollers beneath the sledge. Instead, a man stands near the front of the sledge, pouring water or some other liquid on the ground to reduce friction and make the pulling easier.



When the stone blocks reached the construction site, they had to be lifted to the proper height. That meant, in the later phases of the work, raising blocks weighing many tons by as much as several hundred feet. Flinders Petrie's investigations provided the first real clue to the way this was done, and later archaeologists, examining unfinished pyramids to the south where outlines of the construction work could still be seen, have confirmed his ideas.

No cranes or pulleys were used. After the blocks making up the base of the Great Pyramid were assembled, a sloping ramp of earth was built surrounding the base on all sides. The blocks for the next level were dragged up this earthen ramp by teams of workmen and moved into the positions they were to occupy. Then the ramp was raised, covering the first two levels entirely, and the blocks for the third level were hauled up the slope. The angle of the slope always remained the same as the Pyramid grew; the ramps surrounding the construction stretched farther and farther from the sight as each new level was added. During the construction the Pyramid was completely hidden within this ever-growing blanket of earth, except for the level where the current work was going on. That appeared as a flat stone platform on top of a high dirt mound.

To move the blocks into position at the top of the ramp, the workmen used crowbars and planks. Possibly these were the "machines formed of short wooden planks" that Herodotus mentions, although, as machines go, they were very simple devices indeed. No matter how heavy a block was, it could always be lifted a few inches by a large crew of men wielding crowbars; while one gang tipped the block up, a second crew would slip planks beneath it. Then the other side would be rocked up, more planks would be inserted, and the process would begin again on the first side, until the block stood on a little stack of planks that lifted it to the desired height. Then it could be pushed into its final place.

At last the Pyramid's gilded capstone went on, and the hardest part of the job was over. Now the builders began to apply the outer casing of white limestone, working from the top down. Each block of limestone was hauled up the long, long, sloping ramp by crews of workmen tugging on ropes; it was maneuvered into the proper opening and mortared into place. As they moved downward, the workers removed the construction ramps, so that by the time the bottom row of limestone blocks had been installed the Great Pyramid was free of its temporary earthen covering, and stood shining in the sun.

How long did all this take?

Herodotus says the Great Pyramid demanded the constant labor of one hundred thousand men for twenty years. A visitor looking at those tremendous stone blocks and imagining the effort it must have taken to move them with such primitive methods does not find this estimate difficult to believe. Yet Flinders Petrie and other recent archaeologists think it is a considerable exaggeration. An earlier pyramid located at Dahshur, south of the Gizeh group, bears inscriptions that seem to say that structure was completed in just three years. Since the Dahshur pyramid is only one-third smaller in volume than the Great Pyramid, it appears unlikely that it could have taken almost seven times as long to build Khufu's monument.

Even if it did take twenty years, or not much less, to build the Great Pyramid, Herodotus' statement that one hundred thousand men were kept constantly employed on the job is surely inflated. Herodotus, relying on what the Egyptian guides told him, pictured Khufu as a merciless tyrant who drained the manpower of his nation to build his vast tomb. We find that notion easy to accept, for we are familiar with the Biblical stories of the oppression of the Israelites in the land of Egypt. However, the Pharaoh who supposedly enslaved the children of Israel lived more than a thousand years after Khufu's time. Also, Herodotus visited Egypt at least seven hundred years after the exodus of the Israelites; so Khufu was already a personage out of the remote and myth-shrouded past when Herodotus saw the Great Pyramid, and we must be cautious about believing the tales told of him.

Flinders Petrie did some arithmetic to disprove the numbers supplied by Herodotus. The Greek historian speaks of 100,000-man work forces, each serving for three months; that is, 400,000 workers a year. Since the population of Egypt in Khufu's time was probably not much more than 1,000,000, including women, children, the aged, and the sick, Khufu could not have put together a work force of anything like 400,000 men a year, even if he drafted every able-bodied man in the kingdom.

Nor did he really need so many men. Flinders Petrie calculated that a team of eight men should have been capable of handling the average two-and-a-half-ton block. (The wall painting showing 172 men pulling a 60-ton statue supports this reckoning.) Flinders Petrie argued that if twenty years were spent in building the Great Pyramid, the workers would have had to move 115,000 blocks a year, since there are 2,300,000 in the entire structure. If each eight-man team put one block in place every eight or nine days—which Flinders Petrie regarded as quite possible—it would take about twelve weeks for a working force of 100,000 men to transport and mount the full year's quota of 115,000 blocks. That is, the year's work could conveniently have been done between July and October.

The importance of those months lies in the fact that the Nile, in the days before the existence of the Aswan Dam, overflowed its banks every year between July and October. This was beneficial to Egypt, since the Nile flood cast a thick layer of fertile mud over the fields of the farmers. But during the months of the flood it was impossible to cultivate the fields, and a large portion of the population was forced into idleness. By drafting workmen to serve only during the flood season, Khufu could get a great deal of work done on his Pyramid each year without interfering in any way with the normal output of the Egyptian economy.

During the remaining months of the year a much smaller force of skilled craftsmen may have been employed full-time on the Pyramid—cutting and dressing the stone blocks, building or dismantling the construction ramps, constructing the passageways and chambers inside the Pyramid, and planning the work to be done in the next flood season. Flinders Petrie, excavating near the Pyramid of Khafre, discovered the foundations of the barracks that must have housed these workers; there was room in them for about four thousand men, and Pharaoh's permanent work force probably was no larger than that.

The idea that those who worked on the Great Pyramid must have been downtrodden slaves appears also to be a myth. Slavery, despite the evidence in the Old Testament, was simply not a major feature of life in early Egypt. There were some slaves, usually prisoners of war, but the ordinary Egyptian citizen had definite rights and privileges and could not be forced into backbreaking toil at the casual whim of his monarch.

Nowhere in Egyptian art do we find a picture of struggling laborers groaning under the whips of overseers, although there are plenty of depictions of men at work. The foremen did carry wooden rods, which they probably used to whack a lazy or an unruly worker now and then, but there is no evidence of the sort of brutality that was practiced in other ancient kingdoms. Translations of Egyptian hieroglyphic texts give a similar impression: there are many documents that list the maximum amount of work expected from each laborer each day, the holidays to which he was entitled, and the wages he was to receive. (Since money had not yet been invented, the builders of the Pyramids were paid in food and clothing.) These careful regulations show that Egyptian workers were decently treated, at least by the standards of the ancient world, and that they were far from being the suffering victims of Pharaoh's grandiose schemes that we imagine them to have been.

Of course, the average Egyptian had little choice about whether he would work on the Pyramid. When the flood came and Pharaoh summoned him to the work force, he went, without raising objections. But there is a difference between being a draftee and being a slave. The Egyptian might have preferred to spend the months of flood relaxing, rather than pushing heavy blocks of stone about; but he believed that it was right and proper to build a Pyramid for Pharaoh, and so he put in his time. In the same way, millions of American men let themselves be drafted into the army during the Second World War, not because they liked the idea of being soldiers, but because they believed it was right and proper to fight against the powers of evil that were threatening free men everywhere.

To the Egyptian of 2500 B.C., constructing Khufu's Great Pyramid may well have seemed as important a task as the overthrow of Hitler and his Nazis seemed to the American of A.D. 1943. For the ancient Egyptian was not merely building a tomb for his king; he was erecting a home for his god.

God and king were one in early Egypt. The Pharaoh was a deity in his own lifetime, regarded as a descendant of the sun-god, Re. His subjects hailed him as divine, and worshipped him in temples throughout the land.

A god, when he goes to the afterlife, deserves an imposing tomb. Throughout Egypt's long history it was believed that man's everyday life is only a prelude to what comes after; thus the bodies of dead nobles and kings were carefully embalmed, and these mummies were placed in tombs surrounded by furniture, jewelry, articles of food and clothing, and everything else that they would wish to have in the next world. In prehistoric Egypt, the dead were buried in graves dug in the sand; but about 3200 B.C., the kings and nobles began to have protective brick structures placed over their graves. These platform-shaped coverings are known as *mastabas*, from an Arabic word meaning "bench."

The Pharaohs could not risk letting their descendants build their tombs. To insure the safety of their mummies, they supervised the construction of their eventual resting places while they were still alive; and each Pharaoh strove to outdo all who had gone before him in the magnificence and strength of his own tomb. Mastabas grew bigger and bigger, until, about 2700 B.C., they began to evolve into pyramids.

The man responsible for the change from mastaba to pyramid was Imhotep, grand vizier to Pharaoh Zoser, and the earliest architect whose name we know. Imhotep, an unusually versatile man whom later Egyptians worshipped as a god of learning and medicine, spent many years building, redesigning, and rebuilding a tomb for the future use of his Pharaoh.

He began by constructing Zoser's underground burial-place and covering it by a large mastaba, 26 feet high and 200 feet square. As Zoser's reign continued, Imhotep decided to place a slightly smaller mastaba on top of the first one; then he further enlarged and altered the tomb by adding a third mastaba, a fourth, a fifth and a sixth. In the end the structure formed a kind of terraced pyramid, about 200 feet high, and some 400 by 350 feet at the base; Imhotep covered the whole thing with a layer of limestone blocks to conceal the fact that it was actually a stack of ever-smaller mastabas, but the steplike setbacks of the design remained apparent.

Zoser's successors also had "step pyramids" of this type built for them. But within two centuries the idea of the true pyramid, with smoothly sloping sides and a point at the summit, had taken over. The first Pharaoh to build a pyramid was Seneferu, the father of Khufu.

Seneferu actually built three pyramids. The first, at Meidum, thirty miles south of the ancient Egyptian capital of Memphis, is badly damaged, but seems originally to have been a seven-stepped pyramid that was rebuilt to have eight steps, then covered over with a limestone facing so that its sides would be straight, as in a true pyramid. For some reason Seneferu chose not to use this pyramid, even after all the remodeling, and had a new one built twenty-eight miles to the north, at Dahshur. This time the architects began a true pyramid; but the results, as we see them, are a little strange. Halfway to the top the angle of the slope changes drastically, as though the upper half of a small pyramid had been put down on the base of a large one. Hence this pyramid is known as the Bent Pyramid, or Blunted Pyramid. The upper section is much less carefully constructed than the lower; archaeologists believe that the Bent Pyramid may have been abandoned in the middle by its original architect and completed by much less competent hands. The upper part may even have been built for a later king.

Seneferu's third pyramid, also at Dahshur, is the oldest known true pyramid that was satisfactorily completed. This large pyramid is the one bearing inscriptions that seem to say it was built in only three years. Perhaps the grandeur of Seneferu's final pyramid inspired his son and successor, Khufu, to build his even more splendid monument near Gizeh, in the north.

We do not know the name of Khufu's architect, and probably he employed several of them over the years. For, although the outer shape of the Great Pyramid is impressively perfect, the interior structure shows evidence of several changes in plan.

At first, Khufu's burial chamber was carved out of the rock beneath the Pyramid. As the Pyramid rose, a downward-sloping corridor was left open inside it so that the workmen could get to this chamber. The Descending Corridor, as it is known today, has its entrance about fifty-five feet above ground in the north face of the Great Pyramid and runs hundreds of feet into the structure, down through the lower levels of stone blocks and into the rock below the Pyramid's base. For most of the way this corridor is about four feet high and three and a half feet wide, so that one had to crawl to get through it. It ends in an underground room 11 feet high, 46 feet long, and 27 feet wide—Khufu's original burial chamber.

Perhaps the Pharaoh felt uneasy about being buried here, beneath so many millions of tons of rock. After the work was well along, he or his architects vetoed the idea, and it was decided to abandon the rock chamber and let the Pharaoh's mummy rest within the Pyramid, instead of below it. A new chamber—wrongly called the Queen's Chamber by modern Arab guides—was built into the Pyramid not far above ground level. A second corridor, the Ascending Corridor, leads to it.

We know that plans were changed after work began, for the lower part of the Ascending Corridor had to be cut through blocks of stone that were already in place. The upper part was clearly allowed for in the laying of the stone; it opens into the Queen's Chamber, a room about 18 feet by 17 feet, with a pointed ceiling 20 feet high. This room was still unfinished when Khufu chose to place his burial chamber even higher in the Pyramid.

So the Ascending Corridor was extended upward into the magnificent Grand Gallery, a passageway of complicated form 28 feet high and 153 feet in length. This great open space inside the Pyramid, breathtaking in its beauty and size, provides access to the King's Chamber in the heart of the vast structure. Here is a room fit for the burial of a god-king: a granite-walled chamber 19 feet high, 34 feet long, 17 feet wide, topped by a 400-ton roof. Above it are three small "relieving chambers," built to keep the roof from collapsing under the weight of the Pyramid above it.

Strangely, the King's Chamber is not level with the base of the Pyramid. Flinders Petrie, surveying it in the 1880s, found that the entire room is tilted at one corner; it is 2¼ inches higher on the northeast than the southwest. He found other errors of construction, too, all the more surprising because of the precision with which the outside of the Great Pyramid had been designed. He concluded that a master architect had begun the project, but had not lived to complete it, and that his successors must have been careless, lazy, or lacking in skill.

When Khufu died, his body went through the months-long process of mummification and then was carried into the Great Pyramid for burial. It was taken up the Ascending Corridor and through the Grand Gallery into the King's Chamber, where it was placed in the heavy granite coffin that awaited it. The coffin must have been lowered into the King's Chamber during the construction of the Pyramid, for it is too wide to have been hauled up through the Ascending Corridor.

The massive stone lid was put over the coffin and bolted into place. The funeral procession left the Pyramid; and when everyone else was out, workmen took the final steps that would ensure the unbroken repose of Khufu's mummy through all of time to come. Three huge stone blocks had been propped up near the entrance to the King's Chamber. The workmen knocked the props away, and the blocks crashed down, sealing the entrance. Three more blocks, tremendous cubes of granite, were propped up in the Grand Gallery. The workmen knocked these props away, too, sending the blocks down into the Ascending Corridor to plug it. The workmen found their way out of the Pyramid through a secret shaft connecting the Ascending Corridor to the Descending Corridor, which they closed up as they emerged from it. Now Pharaoh's mummy was safe against intruders; and now there was no chance that thieves might break in to seize the fantastic treasure that had been buried with the body of the dead monarch.

But, of course, intruders did break in and loot the burial chamber.

We do not know when it happened. Perhaps Khufu was allowed to rest in peace for as long as four hundred years. But Egypt entered into a time of troubles about 2100 B.C.; during a long period of confusion and strife the government lost its power, and there was a general breakdown of authority. Often several rival Pharaohs ruled, or claimed to rule, at the same time. In this troubled era it was no longer possible to post guards over the tombs of the old kings, and many of the earlier burial places were broken open and plundered. The Great Pyramid, archaeologists believe, may have been among them.

Certainly the Great Pyramid was entered—if not at that time, then in some later period of unrest and chaos—and the treasures of the Pharaoh, even the mummy itself, were taken. The thieves found a way into the Pyramid through the original entrance by removing the stones that had been used to seal it. They did not disturb the heavy granite plugs blocking the Ascending Corridor, but found some other passageway that led to the King's Chamber. Afterward, the custodians of the Pyramid sealed the entrance and repaired the damage to the outer casing, but it was pointless work; the Great Pyramid had lost its purpose once Khufu's tomb was violated.

In time the robbing of the Pyramid was forgotten, and men came to think that the structure was as it had originally been, with the treasure of the Pharaoh still inside. When Herodotus came, he was told that Khufu lay buried on an artificial island under the Pyramid, and doubtless this is what the Egyptians believed. Now and then, perhaps, attempts were made to break into the Pyramid and find the treasure. The only one of these attempts that we know anything about was made by the Caliph Ma'mun, ruler of the Arab world, in A.D. 818.

Ma'mun, the son of Harun al-Rashid of Arabian Nights fame, persuaded himself that the huge building contained chests heaped with jewels, gold, all the wealth of the ancient king. He ordered workmen to open a passage into the Pyramid. Since all knowledge of the original entrance had been lost, Ma'mun's men hacked a new opening for themselves into the north face, about twenty-five feet below the real entrance. Then, with great effort, they chiseled and smashed their way through the solid blocks for about a hundred feet. The work was so hard and the results so poor that they were about to give up, when a lucky accident gave them a reason to go on.

The builders of the Pyramid had placed a heavy limestone slab across the opening that connected the Ascending Corridor and the Descending Corridor. This was part of the system of plugs designed to block the movements of intruders within the Pyramid. But this slab must not have been firmly fastened, because the hammering of Ma'mun's men caused it to come loose and fall with a terrific crash onto the floor of the Descending Corridor.

As this loud noise echoed through the Pyramid, the startled Arabs realized that they must be in the wrong place. They bored toward the west, heading toward the source of the sound, and soon broke into the Ascending Corridor. Now they raced upward, convinced that the royal coffin could not be far off. When they had gone only a few yards, though, a new obstacle confronted them: one of the colossal granite plugs that blocked the corridor.

They wasted little time at the all but impossible task of drilling through this plug. Instead they dug into the softer limestone of the corridor wall, cutting their own passage around the plug. In this way they detoured past all the granite blocks and burst into the Grand Gallery. From there, they were able to slip past the final plugs that guarded the entrance to the King's Chamber.

By the smoky light of flickering torches they approached the coffin of Khufu. But they were too late—thousands of years too late. The coffin was empty. The treasure of the burial chamber was gone.

As if taking revenge on the Great Pyramid for their disappointment, the Arabs began to mutilate it. For many years after Ma'mun's time they treated it as a handy source for ready-made building blocks. First they carried away the outer casing of lovely limestone to use in their own buildings; then they started to drag down the bigger blocks of the inner structure. They removed about thirty feet from the top of the Pyramid before they gave up. It was just too much trouble to carry away those two-ton blocks of stone. And so they left the remains of Khufu's tomb standing in the desert, plundered and stripped, but still mostly intact. It was a good thing for their descendants that these Arabs of a thousand years ago were too lazy to demolish the whole Pyramid. For now, as in the time of Herodotus, the Great Pyramid of Khufu is one of the world's wonders, and people travel for thousands of miles to see it. Generations of Arabs have earned their living there as guides. They tell much the same stories that Herodotus heard, 2500 years ago; and the tourists listen, and nod, and feel the cold chill of awe as they think of the dedicated toil that must have gone into the building of this man-made mountain of stone, this titanic tomb for a living god.

# 2. The Hanging Gardens of Babylon

Near the city of Baghdad, in Iraq, travelers halt to stare at a vast expanse of broken bricks and crumbling walls, sizzling in the desert sun. This dismal ruin is all that remains of Babylon, once the mightiest city on Earth.

"Alas, alas, that great city," declares the Book of Revelations in the final pages of the New Testament, "that was clothed in fine linen, and purple, and scarlet, and decked with gold, and precious stones, and pearls! For in one hour so great riches is come to nought." And in an earlier section of the Bible, the Book of Jeremiah, it is written, "Thus saith the Lord of hosts, the broad walls of Babylon shall be utterly broken, and her high gates shall be burned with fire; and the people shall labor in vain, and the folk in the fire, and they shall be weary."

By the time the first lists of the Seven Wonders of the World were being drawn up, about 150 B.C., Babylon was already, as Jeremiah says, "heaps, a dwelling place for dragons, an astonishment and a hissing, without an inhabitant." Yet so strong was the memory of this fallen city that two of its features—its walls and its Hanging Gardens—were numbered among the Seven Wonders. (The Walls of Babylon were later dropped from the list and replaced by the Lighthouse of Alexandria.)

The Babylon that contained these wonders was actually the last of many Babylons. Throughout its long history the city was repeatedly destroyed by invaders, rebuilt, destroyed again. For more than twelve centuries it was one of the leading cities of Mesopotamia, "The Land Between the Two Rivers."

The two rivers of Mesopotamia are the Tigris and the Euphrates. On the broad plain between them man's first true civilization arose, perhaps seven thousand years ago. Here, about a thousand miles to the east and north of Egypt, a people called Sumerians came into dominance, began to build cities, to farm, to create a system of writing.

This was even earlier than the rise of civilization in Egypt.

The Sumerians were conquered by invaders about 2400 B.C. — within a century after the completion of the Great Pyramid of Khufu. The new masters of Mesopotamia learned the ways of civilization from those whom they had defeated, and new cities were founded. Among them was Babylon, which by 1800 B.C. was one of the greatest in Mesopotamia. Its ruler then was the famous Hammurabi, whose code of laws has come down to us. Babylon was supreme in the land for many centuries, until challenged by the warlike people of Assyria, in northern Mesopotamia. By 1250 B.C., the Assyrians were strong enough to subdue the Babylonians in battle and make their king a prisoner. Over the next several hundred years the struggle continued, until Babylon was completely overcome and became part of the Assyrian Empire.

During the reign of the bloodthirsty Assyrian Sennacherib (704–681 B.C.) Babylon rebelled. Sennacherib invaded the city and inflicted a terrible revenge on it, which he described in a boastful account that archaeologists have found and translated: "The city and its houses, foundations and walls, I destroyed, I burned with fire. The wall and the outerwall, temples and gods, temple-towers of bricks and earth, as many as there were, I razed and dumped them into the Arahtu canal. Through the midst of that city I dug canals, I flooded its site with water, and the very foundations thereof I destroyed. I made its destruction more complete than by a flood. That in days to come, the site of that city, and its temples and gods, might not be remembered, I completely blotted it out with floods of water and made it like a meadow. . . ."

Nothing was left of ancient Babylon when Sennacherib finished with it. Eight years later, however, this murderous king was slain by his own sons, and in 680 B.C. one of those sons, Esarhaddon, ordered that Babylon be rebuilt. The new Babylon was at first a humble town, only a shadow of what it had been. But it gradually regained its strength and importance. Under Esarhaddon's successors, Assyria weakened and lost its control over the territories it had conquered. By 626 B.C. a native Babylonian prince, Nabopolassar, was able to drive the Assyrians from his city and proclaim the independence of Babylon.

Assyria itself soon fell to the armies of Persia; and Babylon enjoyed a glorious but brief period of reborn magnificence. Under Nabopolassar and his son, Nebuchadnezzar, it became the most marvelous city of its time, outshining in grandeur all other cities of the ancient world.

Nebuchadnezzar, the great builder, came to Babylon's throne in 605 B.C. and ruled for forty-three years. It was he who surrounded the city with its wondrous walls, he who constructed the astonishing temples, avenues, and palaces, he who built the celebrated Hanging Gardens. He led Babylon to dizzying heights of accomplishment; but after his death in 562 B.C., the decline was rapid. He was succeeded by three kings within five years, each weaker than the one before, while the Babylonians abandoned themselves to drinking and lavish parties. In 539 B.C. the city was captured by the troops of Cyrus, king of Persia, who were let into the otherwise impregnable walled city by Babylonian traitors. Though Babylon prospered at first under Persian rule, it revolted in 482 B.C. The Persians harshly put down the revolt, stripped the city of much of its treasure, partly demolished the great walls, and did other damage. Babylon never regained its power; walls and temples and palaces fell into ruins, and the desert gradually engulfed everything. By the sixth century A.D. Babylon was inhabited only by peasants living in flimsy huts, and by the thirteenth century it was entirely abandoned, its vanished glory hidden beneath sand and mud.

Herodotus, naturally, visited Babylon to examine its wonders. He came there about 450 B.C., thirty years after the unsuccessful revolt against the Persians. Though the city had suffered a good deal of harm by then, it was still an awesome sight, and Herodotus described it in terms that later generations found hard to believe.

"In addition to its size," Herodotus wrote, "Babylon surpasses in splendor any city in the known world." He claimed that the fabulous wall surrounding Babylon was 56 miles in length, 80 feet thick, 320 feet high. He said that there was room on top for a four-horse chariot to turn, and that a hundred bronze gates were set in this mammoth wall. Yet this was only the *outer* wall. Within, he said, was "a second inner wall, not so thick as the first, but hardly less strong." He told of fortresses inside the city, of temples that contained immense statues of solid gold, and of many other spectacular features.

For some reason Herodotus did not mention the Hanging Gardens, which three hundred years after his time would be classed among the Seven Wonders of the World. For descriptions of this marvel we must rely on other ancient historians who got their information at second-hand, long after the destruction of Babylon.

It is a little disappointing to realize that the Hanging Gardens of Babylon did not really hang. The name calls up images of some strange structure swinging on long cables, perhaps; but the word "hanging" is merely an inexact translation of the Greek word *kremastos* and the Latin word *pensilis,* by which ancient writers described the gardens. Those words did mean "hanging," but they also could mean "overhanging," in the sense of a balcony or terrace. The Hanging Gardens were, in fact, a sort of penthouse, a roof-garden high above the city, and did not truly "hang" at all.

The story told by several of the ancient historians is that

Nebuchadnezzar built the Hanging Gardens to cheer up his homesick wife, Amyitis, daughter of the king of the Medes. Media, her homeland, was a rugged, mountainous region in Persia. Wishing to ally himself with the king of the Medes, Nebuchadnezzar had married Amyitis and brought her to Babylon, but she could not get used to the flat, dreary, sun-baked countryside around the great city. Seeing that Amyitis was pining for the green, cool, beautiful hills of Media, Nebuchadnezzar resolved to construct a rooftop garden as a kind of artificial mountain for her in Babylon. Trees, shrubs, and flowers would grow on this high terrace; since Babylon rarely received any rain, these would have to be watered by raising water from the Euphrates River, far below. In the lower levels of the structure would be large rooms, kept cool even in the hottest time of the year by water sprinkling down the walls. Through these rooms Queen Amyitis and her court could move, as comfortable as though in cool and lovely Media.

One description of the Hanging Gardens comes from the Greek geographer Strabo, who lived in the first century before Christ. He wrote, "It consists of vaulted terraces, raised one above another, and resting upon cube-shaped pillars. These are hollow and filled with earth to allow trees of the largest size to be planted. The pillars, the vaults, and the terraces are constructed of baked brick and asphalt.

"The ascent to the highest story is by stairs, and at their side are water engines, by means of which persons, appointed expressly for the purpose, are continually employed in raising water from the Euphrates into the garden."

A more detailed account is found in the writings of the Greek historian Diodorus Siculus, who lived at about the same time as Strabo. Diodorus, who believed that the Hanging Gardens were the work of King Cyrus of Persia, wrote, "This garden was four hundred feet square, and the ascent up to it was as to the top of a mountain, and it had buildings and apartments, out of one into another, like unto a theater. Under the steps of the ascent were built arches, one above another, rising gently by degrees, which supported the whole plantation. The highest arch, upon which the platform of the garden was laid, was fifty cubits [80 feet] high, and the garden itself was surrounded with battlements and bulwarks. The walls were made very strong, built at no small charge and expense, being 22 feet thick. . . ."

Diodorus declares that the platform of the garden consisted of huge slabs of stone, covered with a layer of reeds and asphalt, over which were laid tiles, "and over them after all, was a covering with sheets of lead, that the wet which drenched through the earth might not rot the foundation. Upon all these was laid earth of a convenient depth, sufficient for the growth of the greatest trees. When the soil was laid even and smooth, it was planted with all sorts of trees, which both for greatness and beauty might delight the spectators." In one of the rooms underneath the garden were "certain engines" which drew "plenty of water out of the river through certain conduits and contrivances. . . ."

According to Quintus Curtius, who lived in the first century A.D., the Hanging Gardens "equal in height the walls of the town, and their numerous lofty trees afford a grateful shade. The trees are twelve feet in circumference, and fifty feet in height. . . . Supporting these are twenty thick walls, eleven feet distant from each other, surmounted with ranges of stone arches, over which is extended a four-sided pavement of stone, strong enough to bear earth piled high, and water supplied for irrigation. A distant spectator of these groves would suppose them to be woods nodding on their mountains."

If we can believe these stories, the Hanging Gardens must have been stunning to behold: balcony above balcony rising on the palace grounds, to the height of a thirty-story skyscraper, and green trees and plants and vines providing a startling contrast to the harshness of the hot, dusty city below. We can see the Median princess and her ladies in waiting moving happily through the cool, dark suites of rooms, pausing now and again to inhale the scent of flowers or to admire some glossy-leaved shrub. We can hear the clank and clatter of the hidden pumping mechanisms, and the gurgle of river water as it runs into the flower beds far above the streets of Babylon.

Was there ever such a garden? Did the mighty Babylon of Nebuchadnezzar exist, or was it all the product of romantic exaggeration, of taletelling and busy imaginations? Have archaeologists found any proof that these wonders once were real?

Though Babylon had been abandoned, its location had never been forgotten. The shapeless, lumpy mound near Baghdad that concealed its ruins was still known as "Babil" by the natives of the region when the first archaeologists started to work there early in the nineteenth century. They found clay tablets bearing inscriptions in the wedge-shaped cuneiform writing of ancient Mesopotamia, and other evidence that a large city lay in the mound. But Babylon had been built out of bricks made of dried mud, which created a tremendous problem for these pioneers of archaeology. They were unable to tell the mud of brick walls from the mud of debris, and sliced through walls and rubbish alike, not knowing which was which. Not until new techniques were developed for excavating the mud-brick cities of Mesopotamia could Babylon properly be uncovered.

That task fell to the German archaeologist Robert Koldewey, who started work at the mound of Babil in March,

1899. Koldewey, a light-hearted, cheerful man with a sharp sense of humor, had a special gift for the kind of patient toil that was needed to unearth the city of Nebuchadnezzar. It was an enterprise that would occupy him for the next fourteen years.

He had been at work only two weeks when he came upon the tremendous walls of Babylon. After removing tons of debris, he exposed a brick wall 22.4 feet thick. Some 38 feet outside it, there was another wall of brick, 25 feet thick. The space between the walls had been filled with rubble and earth up to the top of the outer wall, forming a continuous surface wide enough for horse-drawn chariots to travel on, and creating what must have seemed to Herodotus like a single wall 80 feet thick. Koldewey measured only 13 miles of wall, against Herodotus' figure of 56 miles, but otherwise the Greek historian's account seemed generally accurate. Babylon had been the most solidly protected city in all the ancient world. No invader could ever break through those walls; the city could fall only by treason from within, as when traitors let the Persian armies enter in 539 B.C.

Within this massive wall, Koldewey found and excavated the immense grand processional roadway that passed from north to south through the heart of the city. This colossal street, 73 feet wide, is perhaps the most majestic ever built in any city of the ancient or the modern world. It was bordered by towering walls, 23 feet high, decorated with brilliantly colored enameled bricks. Every 64 feet along the walls were sculptured lions, red and yellow against a blue background. The road was built of brick, covered with asphalt and then great slabs of white limestone. Lining the sides of the road were slabs of breccia, a soft red and white stone. The edge of each slab, Koldewey discovered, bore this cuneiform inscription:

"Nebuchadnezzar, King of Babylon, son of Nabopolassar, King of Babylon, am I. The Babil Street I paved with Shadu slabs for the procession of the great Lord Marduk. Marduk, Lord, grant eternal life."

Down this handsome boulevard had marched the priests of Babylon's highest god, Marduk. The Babil Street led to the Gate of Ishtar, dedicated to the city's chief goddess. Even today, the Ishtar Gate stands 40 feet high, and it must have been far more imposing in Nebuchadnezzar's day. It was a double gateway, adorned by hundreds of brightly colored bulls and dragons.

Another of Koldewey's finds was a great cube of crumbling brickwork, the base of what once had been the Great Tower of Babylon. The Bible tells of the Tower of Babel, which bold men built so high that it nearly reached God's throne; this was a reference to the *ziggurat,* or sacred tower, found in every Mesopotamian city. The Babylonian ziggurat, set in a great courtyard and surrounded by lesser temples, had been 288 feet high, rising in setback steps. The first stage was 106 feet high, the second 58 feet; then there were four stages of about 19 feet each, topped by a 48-foot-high temple dedicated to the god Marduk. The temple's walls were plated with gold and inlaid with blue enameled bricks, so that the sun, striking the tower's top, illuminated the entire city with a blaze of reflected light. Within the temple, a gold statue of Marduk and golden furniture were kept—twenty-six tons of gold altogether, according to Herodotus. Of all this splendor nothing remained but ruined bricks when Koldewey excavated.

In the northern part of the city, near the Ishtar Gate and just off the grand processional roadway, lay a great mass of ruins that had made up the main fortress of Babylon. Two of these buildings were citadels, planned as additional lines of defense behind the huge wall. Just south of these was a cluster of buildings that Koldewey called the Southern Citadel; here he found the palace of Nebuchadnezzar, the offices of the high government officials, and—perhaps —the remains of the Hanging Gardens.

While working in the Southern Citadel one day, not far from the royal palace, Koldewey came upon a brick staircase leading into a sort of basement. In this cellar he discovered fourteen large rooms whose ceilings were arches of stone. The use of stone at once struck Koldewey as unusual, for stone was scarce in this part of Mesopotamia, and hardly any had been employed in the construction of the rest of the city. In all ancient descriptions of Babylon, only two buildings were said to have been made even partly of stone. These were the Northern Citadel, said to have stone in its north wall, and the Hanging Gardens.

Koldewey had already excavated the north wall of the Northern Citadel, which did indeed contain large quantities of stone. Now he had found a second stone building.

Were these underground arched rooms the basement of the Hanging Gardens?

Koldewey studied the accounts of Diodorus Siculus, Strabo, and the other early writers with great care, seeking to draw from them some picture of how the Hanging Gardens must have looked. Diodorus had told of arches underneath the garden, and of "certain engines" for pumping water located in one of the rooms under these arches. But his account said that the arches were built "one above another, rising gently by degrees." These all were on the same level, covering an area of about 100 feet by 150 feet. The description of Quintus Curtius was closer to what Koldewey beheld: the foundation for the garden consisted of "twenty thick walls, eleven feet distant from each other, surmounted with ranges of stone arches." Nevertheless, Koldewey refused to jump to the conclusion that he had actually found the Hanging Gardens, and continued to dig. He needed more proof; and soon he found it, in one of the western rooms of the arched building, containing a well.

It was a well which, he wrote, "differs from all other wells known either in Babylon or elsewhere in the ancient world. It has three shafts placed close to each other, a square one in the center and oblong ones on each side, an arrangement for which I can see no other explanation than that a mechanical hydraulic machine stood here, which worked on the same principle as our chain pump, where buckets attached to a chain work on a wheel placed over the well. A whim [a shaft with handles] works the wheel in endless rotation. This contrivance, which is used today in this neighborhood, and is called a *dolab* (water bucket), would provide a continuous flow of water."

Now Koldewey was confident of his theory. The stone-arched rooms were the foundation for the gardens, and this basement well was all that remained of the system by which water had been hoisted to the plants above.

Over the arches, Koldewey thought, there must once have been an upper level, or perhaps a whole series of levels, with the garden itself at the top. On the roof of the building would have been a deep layer of earth, in which the garden was planted. The chain of water-buckets went up through the building to the garden; and slaves, pushing the handles of the pump night and day, kept water constantly flowing to Amyitis' beloved plants.

Diodorus Siculus had written of huge slabs of stone that formed the base for the layer of earth; Koldewey found part of this stone roofing in the ruins. It seemed quite likely to him that Diodorus' description of layers of reed and asphalt, tiles, and lead, designed to keep water from seeping through the garden soil into the rooms below, was basically correct. The rooms under the roof garden, said Koldewey, would have been comfortable places of refuge from the fierce heat of the Babylonian summer. "The air that entered the chambers through the leaves of the trees," he wrote, "must have been delightfully cooled by the continuous watering of the vegetation. Possibly the palace officials did a great part of their business in these cool chambers during the heat of the summer." The arched basement rooms underneath everything must have been too dark to use as anything but storehouses, Koldewey said; certain inscriptions found in them indicated that they might have been used for storing grain.

The wonderful Hanging Gardens lose some of their wonder in Koldewey's matter-of-fact reconstruction. "The reason why the Hanging Gardens were ranked among the Seven Wonders of the World," he wrote, "is that they were laid out on the roof of an occupied building." What is wonderful about that? Can these gardens possibly have compared in grandeur with the glittering ziggurat tower and its giant golden statue, or with the grand processional roadway, or with the vast palace of Nebuchadnezzar, or with the noble Ishtar Gate? In this city of wonders, why did the Hanging Gardens attain such fame?

Perhaps for the cleverness of their construction. Grandeur and immensity could be found everywhere; but it was no small thing, in ancient times, to lift water to the top of a large building, and make a grove of greenery flourish seemingly in midair, over sun-blasted Babylon. Then, too, we have no idea what the building looked like; perhaps its leafy terraces and platforms were of extraordinary grace and charm and elegance, so that in truth they appeared to float over the city like something seen in a dream.

A miracle of engineering skill, a marvel of architectural design—possibly these were the qualities that gained the Hanging Gardens of Babylon a place among the Seven Wonders. In this city among cities, astonished visitors turning their eyes toward the rooftops beheld the shining masses of leafy branches, and pointed in awe, and knew that they had seen a sight that all future ages would regard with amazement.

# 3. The Statue of Zeus at Olympia

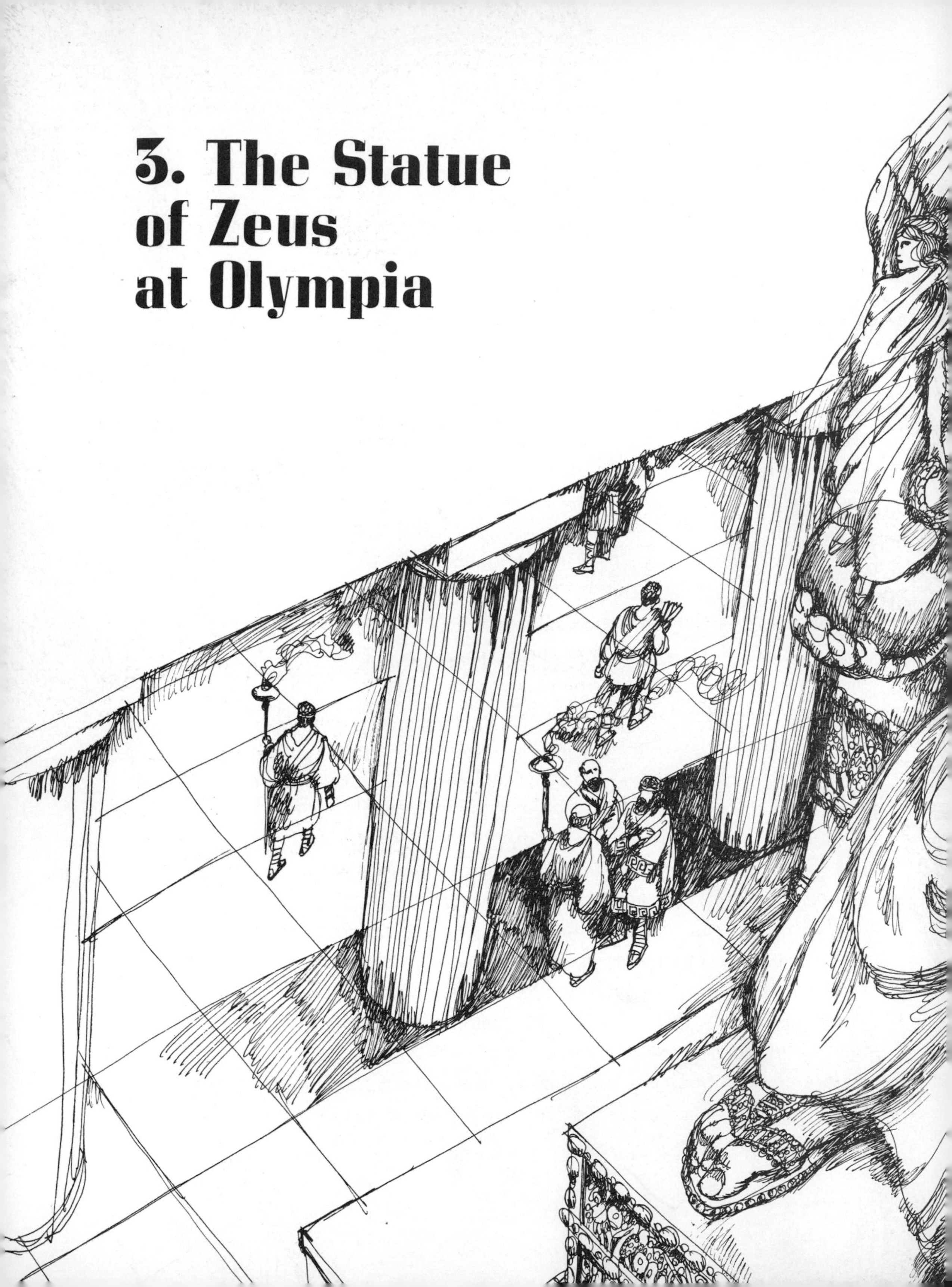

The earliest event in Greek history to which we can give a definite date occurred in 776 B.C. In that year the first Olympic Games took place. The list of winners, covering more than a thousand years, begins there with the name of Coroebus of Elis, who won the foot-race. To the ancient Greeks, the date of Coroebus' victory, signifying the founding of the Olympic Games, was as important an historical marker as such dates as 1492 and 1776 are to us.

Of course, the origins of Greek culture go back far beyond 776 B.C. The Trojan War of which Homer sang—the war in which the Greek heroes Agamemnon, Achilles, Odysseus, Ajax, and the rest conquered the rich city of Troy on the coast of Asia Minor—was fought at least four centuries earlier. The idea of a festival of sacred games, of athletic contests held for a religious purpose, may be even older.

In the *Iliad*, Homer describes the games the Greeks played at the funeral of Achilles' friend Patroclus, in honor of the fallen man. The mourning Greeks contended in a chariot-race, a boxing match, a wrestling match, a foot-race, a discus-throw, and other events. Such sports, Homer makes clear, were quite a normal part of the funeral ceremonies of an important man. Probably they were features of Greek religious festivals from the earliest times; and quite likely the games played at Olympia began several hundred years before the traditional founding date of 776 B.C. It is only an accident of record-keeping that this is the oldest known date for the games.

Olympia, where the Olympics were held every fourth summer, is a place in the northwestern part of the southern peninsula of Greece known as the Peloponnesus. On a sheltered plain bordered by the lofty mountains of the Peloponnesus the Greeks created, about 1000 B.C., a shrine sacred to their chief god, Zeus the Thunderer. All Greeks from every part of the land revered this place, and gathered there regularly to pay homage to Zeus in contests of sport. Gradually, as the importance of Olympia grew, the small early temples there were replaced by grander ones, until in the fifth century B.C. —the greatest century of Greek civilization—a splendid Temple of Zeus was erected, housing a statue that was considered to be one of the Seven Wonders of the World.

The holy shrine of Olympia served as a force to draw the often-divided Greeks together. Greece was not then a nation, but rather a collection of small, independent city-states, usually jealous of their neighbors and quite often at war with them. These bitter conflicts were forgotten only at the time of the sacred games. A truce was proclaimed throughout Greece, so that men of all the rival cities might take part in the games, and so that thousands of Greeks might journey safely to Olympia to be spectators and to worship at the shrine of Zeus.

The Olympic Games were held in high summer at the time of the full moon—that is, in our month of August. The three summers between one set of Olympic Games and the next were occupied by other festivals of games: the Pythian Games, held at Delphi every four years, and the Nemean Games, held at Cleonae every other year. Thus the sequence of games in any five-year period was Olympic, Nemean, Pythian, Nemean again, and then Olympic once more. But the Olympic Games were the oldest and most important of the festivals. The Greeks reckoned time by them, calling each cycle from one Olympic Games to the next an Olympiad, and speaking of an event as having occurred "in the twelfth Olympiad," "in the thirty-fourth Olympiad," or whenever. The first Olympiad was the one beginning in the year we call 776 B.C.

No one actually lived at Olympia except the priests and officials of the shrine. The headquarters for the games was the town of Elis, twenty-five miles northwest of Olympia. In an Olympic year, heralds set forth from Elis some months before the opening of the games, journeying from town to town to proclaim the sacred truce. Thereafter, no matter what wars might be in progress, anyone traveling to Olympia or the region around it was sure of safe passage throughout the season of the games.

The athletes who were going to compete went into training ten months before the opening of the games. Many of them might have been in the previous year's Nemean games, so they would have had only a few months of rest between their exertions. They were required to come to Elis for their final month of training, where they were supervised by officials known as the *hellanodikai,* who saw to it that the games were conducted fairly and honorably. In the three gymnasiums of Elis the athletes sharpened their skills in racing, boxing, wrestling, and gymnastics; the marketplace of the town was turned into a track where the horses to be used in the chariot-races were exercised.

Crowds of spectators pushed into Elis during these last few weeks. Interest in the games was intense, naturally, and both great men and humble came to watch the events. Elis was their first stop; they observed the athletes at their training, feasted at the taverns and hotels, boasted to one another of the great deeds that the men from their native town would perform. Then they moved on to Olympia to pitch their tents near the sacred grove of Zeus. The peaceful shrine would be transformed by this invasion; nearly deserted during the last four years, suddenly it would swarm with peddlers selling food, wine, or souvenirs, with shepherds bringing animals for the sacrifices, with clowns, peasants, princes, retired athletes of other years, priests, philosophers, poets, tradesmen, all those who had come to take part as onlookers in the great festival.

At last the competitors themselves would arrive. Accompanied by the *hellanodikai* and other officials, they came marching out from Elis along the dusty road, under the cruel summer sun, a superb procession of tanned, muscular men. Any Greek citizen could enter the Olympic Games if he wished to; but in practice, only the strongest and most skillful competed. Fear of ridicule, and the high expenses incurred during the training period, kept the less capable athletes away.

The shrine at Olympia had two main sections: the *Altis*, or sacred grove, where the temples were located, and the *Stadion*, or stadium, where the actual games took place. The stadium that visitors to Olympia see today, excavated and carefully restored by archaeologists, was built in the fourth century B.C. Probably this was only the most recent of many stadiums built on the same site over a period of three or four centuries as the Greeks expanded and redesigned their Olympic shrine. Archaeologists have found that in the early years the stadium opened directly onto the Altis, so the athletes could perform in sight of the great temples; but during its final rebuilding, about 350 B.C., a long, columned building known as the Echo Colonnade was added along the east side of the Altis, cutting it off from the stadium.

A covered passageway connected the Altis to the stadium after the Echo Colonnade's construction. Through this passageway came the athletes and the *hellanodikai* at the beginning of the games. Most of the spectators sat on the ground, which was graded in levels going up the side of a hill at the north end of the stadium. On the south end were stone seats where the chief judges sat. After the construction of the Echo Colonnade, other high officials of the shrine and the most distinguished visitors were able to watch the games from the comfort of a lounge within this building, where they were sheltered from heat or rain.

The festival lasted five days. On the first day, the athletes were questioned to make sure they were citizens, and hence eligible to compete. Those who passed this scrutiny swore to abide by the principles of the Olympic Games. The judges, too, took oaths that day, vowing to accept no bribes, to give fair decisions, and to keep secret the reasons for their decisions.

On the second day, the stadium was the scene of the pentathlon, a five-part competition designed to test the all-around skills of the athletes. The pentathlon consisted of a foot-race, a jumping contest, wrestling, and throwing the discus and javelin; the athlete who excelled in the greatest number of categories was the winner. Rhythm and grace were as important as strength; several of the events were accompanied by the music of the flute, to inspire in the competitors the proper harmony of movements. The rules required the athletes to compete in the nude, for the Greeks did not regard a handsome naked body as a shameful thing, and clothing was only a hindrance in the contests. (The word *gymnasium* literally means "a place where one exercises in the nude." *Gymnos* is the Greek word for "naked.")

When all five events were played, the judges announced the grand winner of the pentathlon, and heralds with trumpets called forth his name, that of his father and of his city. Olympic winners received as their prizes nothing more than a crown fashioned from the boughs of a wild olive tree. With that simple crown went tremendous prestige, particularly if the winner came from one of the smaller cities. When he returned home, he would receive a hero's welcome, and for the rest of his life he would be hailed as the man who had brought honor to his family and to his city by his triumph at Olympia.

Also on the second day, the chariot races and other horse racing events were held at the Hippodrome, south of the stadium by the banks of the Alpheus River. Nothing remains of the Hippodrome today, for it was long ago destroyed by floods and buried deep under river mud. The high point of this competition was the four-horse chariot race, in which professional drivers were allowed to compete, at least in later years; important Greek political figures frequently entered this event, buying the chariot, hiring the best drivers available, and taking credit and glory for victory just as though they had competed in person.

The third day, the day of the full moon, was set aside for a high religious ceremony: the sacrifice to Zeus in the main temple. The only games that day were events for boys, played in the afternoon. The next day saw the chief individual events: foot-races in the morning, wrestling, boxing, and *pankration* (a free-for-all combination of boxing and wrestling) in the afternoon. These events were held in the stadium.

Most of the excitement centered about the foot-races. Marble blocks marked the start and finish of the racecourse. These blocks were placed one *stade,* or 600 Olympic feet, apart. The Olympic foot was somewhat longer than the unit we use today—it spanned about thirteen modern inches—and differed also from the foot that was in use at other Greek cities in ancient times. The stade was about 630 modern feet in length.

The main event was the one-stade race, a quick dash from one marble block to the other. The course was wide enough for some twenty runners at a time. In addition there was a two-stade race; a long-distance race of varying length that might be as much as twenty-four stades or almost three miles; and a two-stade race in armor.

The winners celebrated their victories by hanging trophies of armor on the embankments above the track. From time to time these embankments were raised, and any trophies on display were buried; new gifts of armor were hung at the higher levels of the embankments. In this way, over the centuries, the area around the track came to hold a superb collection of Greek armor, much of which has been found by archaeologists. The museum at Olympia houses the largest such collection in the world, showing the changes in armor style through the years. Also discovered near the stadium were inscriptions of poems in honor of certain winners, and such things as a 316-pound block of red sandstone on which it is written that an athlete named Bybon lifted the block over his head with one hand. Near the entrance to the stadium stood bronze statues of Zeus, built with money raised by fining athletes who broke the Olympic rules. The bases of sixteen of these statues have been found; there must have been many more in the days when the contests flourished.

The fifth day of the festival was devoted to feasts and celebrations. Then the peddlers' booths and the spectators' tents were taken down, the olive-wreathed victors started home for further honors, and the disappointed losers began to make plans for next year's Nemean Games. The grand holiday was over.

The five days of the Olympic Games were more than simply a time of athletics and carousing, however. This was, after all, the high festival of Greece's most important god, and the temples of the Altis, no less than the stadium and the Hippodrome, were the scenes of much activity. There were two main temples, one to Zeus and one to his wife Hera, and a variety of lesser shrines.

The Temple of Hera was the oldest building at Olympia and one of the oldest temples in all of Greece. Originally it served as a Temple of Hera and Zeus, until the construction of a separate temple for Zeus. No doubt from the earliest days of the festival at Olympia there was some kind of temple where this one now stands, but the present

Temple of Hera, as uncovered by archaeologists, was begun in the eighth century B.C., was twice rebuilt, and took its final form around 600 B.C. It was a long, narrow building, with sixteen columns along its sides and six at each end. The columns are in many styles, because they were at first made of wood, and were replaced in stone over many years; as late as the second century A.D. there still was one wooden column in the back porch.

Greek temples generally contained nothing except a large statue of the god or goddess to whom the temple was dedicated. The Greeks valued simplicity above most other virtues, and disliked filling their temples with a clutter of religious objects. (The Lincoln Memorial, in Washington, D.C., gives us some idea of how a major Greek temple must have looked.) Pausanias, a Greek geographer of the second century A.D. who saw the Temple of Hera before its destruction, wrote that within it was an image of Hera seated upon a throne, with an image of Zeus standing beside her. Of this nothing remains except the head of Hera, which archaeologists have found. Pausanias also mentioned a statue of Hermes, the messenger god, carrying the young god of revelry, Dionysus. This statue, unearthed in the ruins in 1877, now can be seen in the museum at Olympia.

For centuries this temple served the needs of all who came to worship at Olympia; but in the fifth century B.C., Zeus received a temple of his own, one of the greatest and most splendid the Greeks ever erected. Pausanias says that the Temple of Zeus at Olympia was built by the citizens of Elis and paid for with the booty they seized by invading and conquering the rival town of Pisa. The temple was begun between 470 and 460 B.C., and probably was completed about 456 B.C. Libon of Elis was the architect's name; we know little else about him, but on the evidence of this one work, he must have been a master.

The Temple of Zeus rose on a high platform, and dominated the grove of the Altis. Thirteen heavy columns ran along each side, and six on each end, supporting a gently sloping roof of white marble. Though the Greeks loved simplicity within their temples, the outsides were a different matter, and the exterior of the Temple of Zeus was richly decorated. Not only was the whiteness of the plaster-covered limestone ornamented by painted areas of red and blue, but elaborate sculptures covered most of the building's outer surface.

The most celebrated of these sculptures were those on the temple's two pediments—the triangular areas above the columns at each end of the building. Each of these pediments showed a scene out of Greek mythology, one calm and dignified, one violent and strenuous. The eastern pediment of a Greek temple was above the front entrance, and by tradition was supposed to show a stately, quiet scene. The episode chosen by the unknown artist met this requirement, although it was drawn from one of the least attractive of the Greek tales, that of Pelops and Oenomaus.

Pelops, a legendary king in Asia Minor, was driven from his home by barbarians and crossed the Aegean Sea to the Greek mainland with a great horde of followers. He came to Olympia and asked to marry Hippodameia, the daughter of King Oenomaus, who ruled over the cities of Elis and Pisa.

Oenomaus had been warned by a prophet that the man who married his daughter would kill him; and so he had devised a grim way to keep Hippodameia unwed. Whoever wished to marry her would first have to engage in a chariot race with her father. If the suitor won, he could have Hippodameia and kill Oenomaus; but if Oenomaus won, the suitor must die. Oenomaus was willing to give each suitor a half-hour head start, while he performed a sacrifice at the altar of Zeus at Olympia. Nevertheless, he was confident of overtaking all who challenged him, for his chariot was specially designed for racing; his driver, Myrtilus, was the best in Greece; and his horses, gifts of the god of war, Ares, were the swiftest in the world.

Thus Oenomaus disposed of thirteen suitors, spearing each one, beheading them, and nailing their heads above the gates of his palace. Pelops, though, bribed the charioteer Myrtilus to betray his master. The scene on the east pediment of the Temple of Zeus shows the contestants preparing for the fatal race. Just before it was to begin, Myrtilus treacherously removed the pins from the axle of Oenomaus' chariot, replacing them with pins made of wax. Then the chariot of Pelops sped away along the course Oenomaus had laid out.

After making his sacrifice at Olympia, Oenomaus set out, and soon his miraculous chariot had caught up with that of Pelops. As Myrtilus urged the horses on, Oenomaus rose in the chariot, grasping his spear, and made ready to thrust it into Pelops' back. At that moment the waxen pins gave way; the axle and wheels of Oenomaus' chariot fell off; Oenomaus was caught in the wreckage and dragged to his death. Pelops then slew Myrtilus to prevent him from revealing the story. Afterward, Pelops conquered the entire region, which he named after himself as the Peloponnesus or "island of Pelops," and became the most powerful ruler in Greece; among his descendants was Agamemnon, the commander-in-chief of the Greek army in the Trojan War.

This somber story of deceit and murder seems an unlikely thing to place on the pediment of a temple. But Pelops was one of the heroes of the Olympic Games; the chariot race of the games was said to be a re-enactment of his race with Oenomaus, and sacrifices in honor of Pelops were always made at the opening of each festival. The quiet beauty of the eastern pediment, showing the charioteers readying themselves, summoned up the spirit of the Olympic Games more than it did the terrible events of the story being depicted.

The western pediment of a Greek temple, over the rear entrance, customarily showed a scene of action. The one used at Olympia portrayed the battle between the Centaurs and the Lapiths, a mountain tribe of northern Greece. The king of the Lapiths had invited the Centaurs, a race of creatures that were half men, half horses, to his marriage feast. The Centaurs became drunk and tried to kidnap the bride, touching off a wild struggle that the Lapiths finally won. The pediment scene showed eight figures, taut and straining in conflict. In one corner a kneeling Lapith fought with a Centaur who was trying to carry off a Lapith woman. In the middle a Centaur and a Lapith battled, and in the other corner a Lapith aimed a weapon at a Centaur gripping an angry Lapith woman.

There were other sculptures along the outside of the building as well. Below the pediments, but above the supporting columns, the twelve labors of Heracles were shown, six at each end. These contrasted sharply with the pediment sculptures, for underneath the violent Centaur-Lapith pediment are six serene images of Heracles at rest after his labors, and below the quiet Pelops-Oenomaus pediment are six portrayals of Heracles in action.

The supreme artistic achievement of the Temple of Zeus at Olympia was within it: the monumental statue of Zeus, which by itself was considered one of the Seven Wonders of the World. For more than twenty years after its completion, the inner hall of the temple stood empty, awaiting this mighty work of art. Phidias of Athens, whom the Greeks deemed the greatest of their sculptors, was its creator.

Phidias was a friend of Pericles, who ruled Athens during its golden age of art and philosophy in the fifth century B.C. When Pericles came to power in 449 B.C., he commenced a program of building temples and shrines atop the Acropolis, the hill that looks down on Athens, and gave Phidias charge of all sculpture. Phidias devoted his finest efforts to the Parthenon, the temple dedicated to Athena, goddess of Athens. For the main hall of the Parthenon he produced a gold-and-ivory statue of Athena forty feet high. One ancient writer said of it, "A man heavy-laden, who had drained the cup of misfortune and sorrow, if he were to stand and gaze at this statue, would forget the heavy and weary weight of this unintelligible world." In addition, Phidias designed the sculptures for the pediments of the temple, showing scenes from the myths of Athena, as well as the sculptures for the temple's other outer surfaces.

The statue of Athena was dedicated in 438 B.C. Soon after, Phidias journeyed to Elis to discuss an assignment to fashion an even more majestic statue for the Temple of Zeus at Olympia. He set up a workshop west of the temple and spent several years at the job.

Since the statue was destroyed long ago, we must rely on ancient writers for knowledge of it. From Pausanias, who saw it more than six hundred years after it was made, we know that it stood at the west end of the temple's great central hall, that it rested on a stone pedestal 3 feet high and 22 feet wide, and that it was nearly 40 feet tall, so that the head of Zeus must have been close to the roof. Like the statue of Athena in the Parthenon, it was made of ivory and plates of gold, fastened to a framework of wood. This material is called *chryselephantine,* derived from the Greek words for gold and ivory. The climate of Olympia is a damp one most of the year, and the statue required special care so that the humidity would not cause the ivory to crack; it was regularly treated with oil kept in a pool in the temple floor, and for centuries the descendants of Phidias held the responsibility of oiling the statue.

As the largest and most majestic figure of the most important of the gods, the Zeus of Olympia inspired tremendous awe in all who beheld it. Quintilian, a Roman writer of the first century A.D., declared, "Its beauty can be said to have added something to traditional religion." Zeus was depicted seated on a huge golden throne, in which were set ebony, ivory, and precious stones. In his uplifted right hand he held a figurine of Nike, the goddess of victory; in his left was a scepter inlaid with precious metals, on which an eagle rested. His feet, clad in richly decorated sandals, rested on a golden footstool that reached the eye-level of the worshippers. A mantle of gold flowed across his ivory shoulders. His face, calm, commanding, bearded, was beyond any doubt the face of an all-powerful deity.

The effect must have been overwhelming. To the Greeks, art was an essential part of religion; and here in Olympia, art and religion became one in the figure of this gigantic Zeus, at once so noble, so godlike, and so magnificently executed. One philosopher declared that it was among the greatest of misfortunes to have died without seeing it.

When his work was done, Phidias returned to Athens, where he fell into political difficulties. Pericles, his friend and patron, had acquired many enemies during his long rule; and since those enemies had no way of openly attacking Pericles, they aimed their fire at those who were close to him. Phidias was arrested on a charge of having stolen some of the gold intended for Athena's statue in the Parthenon. When he proved that this was false, he was accused on a different count. In one of the Parthenon statues, that of Athena bearing a shield, it appeared that the faces of Phidias and Pericles could be seen among the figures decorating the shield. If Phidias had indeed carved his own image and that of his friend onto the temple, he was guilty of impiety; and he was placed in prison, where he died, shrouded in scandal, while awaiting trial.

His two masterworks of Athens and Olympia lived after him for centuries. The statue of Athena may have remained intact until the fifth century A.D.; but then it was destroyed, apparently, when the Parthenon was converted into a Christian church.

The statue of Zeus at Olympia had a similar fate. The Olympic Games continued long after Greece itself had fallen from glory and had become part of the Roman Empire; and the pilgrimages to the wondrous shrine of Zeus continued well into the Christian era. In A.D. 267, barbarian invaders did serious damage to many of the buildings at Olympia, but the Temple of Zeus survived, and fragments of the ruined buildings were used to build a wall around the inner part of the shrine. The list of Olympic winners ends in A.D. 385 with the name of an Armenian prince, Varazdates, who won the boxing match. Eight years later, in the 293rd Olympiad, the games were officially abolished by Emperor Theodosius I of Rome, who was a Christian and sought to wipe out all remnants of the pagan world. Early in the fifth century, Emperor Theodosius II went further: he had the statue of Zeus smashed to pieces and the temple destroyed. An earthquake some time later finished the job of demolishing the sanctuary at Olympia.

Some fourteen centuries later, in 1829, the Greeks were struggling for their independence against the Turks, who had conquered them in medieval times. A French task force went to Greece to assist them in their fight; and with the French came a few archaeologists, who conducted the first excavations at Olympia. They traced the outlines of the ruined Temple of Zeus, and unearthed fragments of three of the sculptures showing the labors of Heracles.

These were taken back to Paris, where they now are on display at the Louvre Museum.

In 1875, a German archaeological expedition arrived for the first of five summers of work. Using Pausanias as their guide, they were able to identify nearly every building of the Altis, and to work out an accurate plan of the entire shrine. They discovered more fragments of the Heracles sculptures, and the chariots from the pediment sculpture of Pelops and Oenomaus. East of the shattered temple they came upon some fragments of the great Zeus statue; at the other side lay carvings of Lapiths and Centaurs.

Clearing the temple floor, the Germans found the place where the pedestal of Zeus had been, and the sunken rectangle in the floor that had contained the oil for preserving the statue. They dug also in the stadium area, where in their final season they discovered the marble starting blocks of the racecourse.

In 1896 the Olympic Games were revived, chiefly through the efforts of a French scholar who hoped that the friendly rivalry of international athletics would serve to unite the nations of the world. The first modern Olympics were held at Athens, in a new marble stadium built for the purpose; in 1900 they took place in Paris, in 1904 in St. Louis, in 1908 in London, and so on every four years thereafter, except during the two world wars. Since 1936, the games have opened with the lighting of a sacred Olympic flame at the stadium; the flame is kindled at Olympia, and carried by relays of runners to the place where the games of each Olympiad are being held.

The 1936 games were held in Berlin, and resulted in a revival of the interest of German archaeologists in Olympia. They returned there in 1937, after a lapse of more than fifty years; the work was conducted on a much larger scale than ever before, with the intention of completely uncovering and restoring the stadium and of surveying the other buildings as thoroughly as possible. The project was interrupted in 1942 by World War II, and not begun again for ten years. By 1960 the stadium was entirely cleared, and a year later had been restored to its appearance as of the fourth century B.C.

During the course of these recent Olympia excavations, the site of the workshop of Phidias was discovered. Pausanias had said that this workshop lay west of the Temple of Zeus. In 1876, the first German archaeologists had noticed the ruins of an ancient building there, beneath an early Christian church. Between 1954 and 1958, digging in and around the church revealed that it did indeed cover the great sculptor's workshop. The archaeologists found a pit for bronze-casting, bits of paint and modeling plaster, sculptors' tools, slivers of ivory, even part of an elephant's tusk from which ivory had been cut. Most important was a series of heavy clay molds that had been used for the statue of Zeus. These were reinforced with iron rods, and had served to support the thin sheets of gold that were hammered to form the statue's drapery. Some bore serial letters on the back to show their place in the pattern.

The pottery found in the workshop helped to settle a question that historians had long debated: had Phidias done the statue of Zeus before or after the statue of Athena in the Parthenon? His Athena, it was definitely known, had been dedicated in 438 B.C. The style of pottery in the workshop could be dated to about 430 B.C. Thus the Zeus of Olympia was the last great work of Phidias, the crowning achievement of his career and a fitting candidate for the roster of the wonders of the ancient world.

There was no doubt, by the way, whose workshop this had been. One of the pieces of pottery discovered by the archaeologists was neatly labeled on its bottom: "I belong to Phidias."

# 4. The Temple of Artemis at Ephesus

The Biblical Book of Acts tells of the uproar created in the city of Ephesus in Asia Minor when the Apostle Paul attempted to convert its people to the new religion of Christianity. Paul came to Ephesus about A.D. 57, when the followers of Jesus were few in number. At that time Ephesus was the center of an ancient and powerful belief centering around the goddess Diana, also known as Artemis. The worship of this goddess was an important business for the Ephesians; as long as men could remember, pilgrims had come there to pay homage at her famous temple, and the prosperity of the city depended on the money that they spent there for food, lodging, and silver statuettes of the goddess. Paul proceeded to work miracles, healing the sick and driving out evil spirits, and gained many converts to Christianity. Then, the New Testament declares, a certain man named Demetrius, whose craft it was to make the silver idols of the goddess, called others of his trade together to discuss the situation, and said:

"Sirs, ye know that by this craft we have our wealth.

"Moreover ye see and hear, that not alone at Ephesus, but almost throughout all Asia, this Paul hath persuaded and turned away much people, saying that they be no gods, which are made with hands:

"So that not only this our craft is in danger to be set at nought; but also that the temple of the great goddess Diana should be despised, and her magnificence should be destroyed, whom all Asia and the world worshippeth.

"And when they heard these sayings, they were full of wrath, and cried out, saying, Great is Diana of the Ephesians."

*Great is Diana of the Ephesians!* It was the cry of angry men, defending their goddess, their temple, and their livelihoods against the preachings of this stranger, Paul. But what did they have to fear? Could the followers of a crucified Palestinian prophet ever hope to turn the hearts of men away from Diana of the Ephesians? Was her religion not one of the oldest and most powerful on earth? Was not her temple at Ephesus one of the Seven Wonders of the World?

*The Temple of Artemis at Ephesus*

"I have seen the walls and Hanging Gardens of ancient Babylon," says the book on the Seven Wonders credited to Philon of Byzantium, "the statue of Olympian Zeus, the Colossus of Rhodes, the mighty work of the high Pyramids, and the tomb of Mausolus. But when I saw the temple at Ephesus rising to the clouds, all these other wonders were put in the shade." Pausanias, too, wrote that this temple surpassed all other structures built by human hands. Yet the Temple of Artemis at Ephesus is long gone; the goddess has no worshippers; the silversmiths ceased centuries ago to fashion images of her; Ephesus itself is a muddy, unimportant Turkish village. And the religion Paul preached still lives.

Ephesus was one of the many colonies founded by the Greeks along the coast of Asia Minor, just across the Aegean Sea from Greece itself. According to a local legend, the first colonists arrived in 1087 B.C., and very likely the city actually was founded about that time.

The goddess of Ephesus, Artemis, was not the same as the goddess of that name worshipped on the Greek mainland. The Artemis of Greece, who later became identified with the Roman goddess Diana, was the deity of hunting, a slim, athletic young woman armed with bow and arrow. But Artemis of Ephesus ("Diana of the Ephesians," in the New Testament) was a mother-goddess, the deity of fertility. In the Vatican Museum in Rome there is a statue of this Artemis, probably patterned after the ones that Demetrius and his fellow silversmiths were turning out at the time of St. Paul's visit. It is a strange figure that might almost represent a creature from some other world: a woman with her arms upraised, the lower half of her body tightly wrapped in clothing, the upper half covered with breasts from the shoulders to the hips. These dozens of breasts are thought to symbolize Artemis' role as a goddess of fertility. Some scholars believe that originally the statue was draped with eggs or clusters of dates, which later artists transformed into breasts.

There is nothing Greek about the style of this bizarre statue. Quite possibly Artemis of Ephesus was a divinity of the primitive inhabitants of Asia Minor, whose cult the Greek colonists adopted when they moved in.

A shrine of Artemis was in existence at Ephesus at least as early as 800 B.C., on marshy ground along a river near the town. Here the sacred stone of Artemis was kept, "the image which fell down from Jupiter," as the Book of Acts calls it—probably a meteorite. About 660 B.C., a tribe of barbarians known as the Cimmerians swept through Asia Minor, invading Ephesus and destroying the shrine. It was rebuilt, destroyed again, and built a third time in 600 B.C. By now Ephesus was a major city, and this temple was a large one, with handsome stone columns. The architect, Chersiphron, feared that the carts carrying these columns to the temple site would become mired in the marshy ground, so he devised a clever way of transporting them. He laid the columns on their sides and hitched teams of oxen to them; the oxen pulled the columns along the ground like huge lawn-rollers.

About 550 B.C., Ephesus was attacked by Croesus, king of Lydia, another region of Asia Minor. Croesus—famous in Greek myths for his great wealth—made Ephesus his first victim in a campaign of conquest by which he became master of all the Greek cities of Asia Minor. Apparently the temple designed by Chersiphron was destroyed during this war, for Croesus celebrated his triumph over Ephesus by contributing generously to a splendid new temple in honor of the city's goddess.

Croesus' temple was a structure of white marble, remarkable for its size. It was 300 feet in length, 150 feet in width—four times as big as the temple it replaced. More than one hundred enormous stone columns, arranged in a double row all around the building, supported its massive roof. Though huge, these columns were slender in proportion to their height, and gave an impression of unusual grace and lightness. A lavish use of sculptured decoration was a distinctive feature of the temple; even the columns were adorned with carvings, which was uncommon in Greek architecture.

The empire assembled by Croesus passed into the hands of Cyrus, king of Persia, and for the next century Ephesus was part of the Persian Empire. After 454 B.C. it came under the control of Athens; later it took the side of Sparta in the bitter war between Athens and Sparta that served to shatter Greek civilization, and by 387 B.C. it was once more subject to the Persians. During these years of changing masters, the Ephesians managed to flourish and exand, and their giant temple was one of their proudest treasures until its destruction in 356 B.C.

The architect who planned that temple is thought to have been an engineer named Theodorus; we are not sure of that, but we do know the man responsible for its ruin. He was a young Ephesian named Herostratus, who wanted his name to live through the ages, and who could find no better way to gain the immortality he craved than to burn down his city's temple. And so it happened. The Ephesians, horrified at his deed, decreed that anyone who mentioned the name of Herostratus should be put to death; but this decree itself served to spread the story more widely, and guaranteed Herostratus the fame he had won in such an evil fashion.

Shortly afterward the Ephesians began to rebuild their temple, on the same site and with virtually the same plan as the one that had been burned. It was this new Temple of Artemis that was reckoned among the Seven Wonders of the World. Ephesus was now one of the greatest cities of Asia Minor, a rich port of some two hundred thousand people, with walls eight miles around, and a harbor thronged with ships of many lands. No expense was spared to make the new temple the most magnificent ever constructed. The rulers of many other cities of Asia Minor sent contributions, out of respect to Artemis; the finest architects and sculptors were hired; the most luxurious materials were used. Scopas of Paros, the outstanding sculptor of his day, was placed in charge of the entire project.

Most of the information we have concerning this last and greatest Temple of Artemis at Ephesus comes from the writings of Pliny the Elder, a Roman naturalist and historian who lived from A.D. 23 to 79. (He was killed while observing the eruption of Mount Vesuvius that buried the city of Pompeii.) Pliny tells us that the temple was "the most wonderful monument of Grecian magnificence, and one that merits our genuine admiration." The Ephesians, he explains, always built and rebuilt their temple in a marshy place, "in order that it might not suffer from earthquakes, or the chasms which they produce. On the other hand, so that the foundations of so vast a pile might not have to rest upon a loose and shifting bed, layers of trodden charcoal were placed beneath, with fleeces covered with wool upon the top of them," when the last of the temples was built.

These precautions raised the floor level of the temple seven feet above the level of the old temple of Croesus, and the area of the floor was also increased. "The entire length of the temple," Pliny wrote, "is 425 feet, and the width 225 feet. The columns are 127 in number, and 60 feet in height, each of them presented by a different king.

36 of these columns are carved, and one of them by the hand of Scopas." (The Parthenon in Athens, which now is the best known of the Greek temples, was 230 feet long, 100 feet wide, and had 58 marble columns, each 34 feet high.)

The roof of the building, according to Pliny, "is wholly constructed of planks of cedar." He quotes a certain Mucianus as reporting that "the doors are made of cypress, and the wood, which has now lasted very nearly four hundred years, has all the appearance of new." Within the temple was a statue of Artemis, made of wood, which at some point had taken the place of the meteorite in the original shrine. "All the writers say that it is ebony," Pliny comments, "with the exception of Mucianus, who . . . declares that it is made of the wood of the vine, and that it has never been changed all the seven times that the temple has been rebuilt." A staircase leading to the roof of the temple, says Pliny, was "constructed of a single vine, that was brought from Cyprus; the vines of that island often attaining a most remarkable size."

Pliny also discusses the problems encountered by the architect when putting the heavy stone-supporting beams of the roof in place atop the columns. This was managed, he says, by making a sloping ramp of sandbags that were piled higher than the tops of the columns. The big beams were hauled to the top of this ramp; then the lower sandbags gradually were emptied, allowing the beams to settle into their correct places. This worked well enough, Pliny says, except for the lintel, the horizontal slab to be placed over the main entrance to bear the weight of the roof: "It was an enormous mass of stone, and by no possibility could it be brought to lie level upon the jambs which formed its bed; in consequence of which, the architect was driven to such a state of anxiety and desperaiton as to contemplate suicide. Wearied and quite worn out by such thoughts as these, during the night, they say, he beheld in a dream the goddess in honor of whom the temple was being erected; she exhorted him to live on, saying that she herself had placed the stone in its proper position. And such, in fact, next morning, was found to be the case; the stone's own weight had apparently brought it to the proper level."

Construction of this immense building took many years; Pliny says 120 years were needed, although the actual figure was probably about half that. The work was still unfinished in 333 B.C. when Alexander the Great of Macedon arrived at Ephesus. Alexander, who was heading east to conquer Persia, freed the Greek towns of Asia Minor from Persian rule; and he had a special interest in Ephesus, for he had been born on the night in 356 B.C. when Herostratus set fire to the old temple. After he had liberated Ephesus, Alexander offered to pay the remaining cost of the new temple, if the Ephesians would carve his name upon it as its builder. This was an awkward request, but the Ephesians found a tactful and flattering way of refusing it. "It is not fitting," they said, "that one god should build a temple for another god." Alexander, pleased, let the matter drop.

The completed temple was enrolled among the Seven Wonders of the World, perhaps for its extraordinary size and for the beauty of the sculptures and paintings it contained. It was far more ornately decorated than other Greek temples, and did not represent the true Greek taste —for Ephesus, though Greek in language and origin, was an Asian city by location and cultural background, and some mingling of styles was unavoidable. If it existed today, we might think less of the Temple of Artemis than we do of the smaller, simpler, Parthenon. But in ancient times the splendor and magnificence of the Ephesian temple made it the better known structure.

Its glory endured for many centuries. In 133 B.C., Ephesus

became part of the Roman Empire, and the Romans greatly enlarged the city, which for a while was the most prosperous in that part of Asia. When St. Paul came there, about A.D. 57, the cult of Artemis was as popular as ever, and had found followers even in Rome itself. But the new creed of Jesus was destined to prevail. The Christians, a persecuted minority at first, gradually gained in strength, and the worshippers of "Diana of the Ephesians" grew ever fewer.

In the year 262, the Goths, one of the many barbaric tribes roaming Europe and Asia Minor, plundered and burned Ephesus and its temple. This time no one thought of rebuilding the ruined wonder, for the old religion was dying. Constantine, the great fourth-century Roman emperor, erected a number of handsome new buildings at Ephesus, but he left the gutted temple to crumble; Constantine was a Christian and had no interest in restoring pagan shrines. In the years that followed the Ephesians used the temple as a quarry, tearing off the roof and uprooting the columns to serve as construction materials. The sculptures that had awed the ancient world were pounded up to make lime for wall plaster.

One sacred image escaped the destruction, however: a lifesize marble statue of Artemis, perhaps a copy of the one that had been venerated in the temple for so long. About the year A.D. 400, it was buried under the floor of the town hall of Ephesus, possibly by the last worshippers of the goddess, who wished to protect it from the hammers of the Christians. There it remained until 1956, when it was discovered by Austrian archaeologists. The goddess wears an intricate headdress ornamented with the images of animals; across her chest are carved the signs of the Zodiac; and below them are not rows of breasts, as on the better-known Vatican statue, but rows of eggs, likewise symbolizing fertility.

Christian Ephesus turned its back on its ancient religious heritage. In the fifth century a fine new temple arose there, but this was a Christian church, dedicated to the Virgin Mary. An important conference of church leaders was held there in A.D. 431.

Soon, though, Ephesus entered into its final decline. The marble walls and towers were gone. The river that ran by the city filled the harbor with silt, and the inhabitants lacked the energy to dredge it clear; the port choked to death as the silt reached sea level, and trees sprouted on the new land. In the end Ephesus, once a mighty maritime city, found itself three miles from the coast. Malaria drove the remaining Ephesians out of their marshy plain, into the mountains to the east; only a few hundred diehards remained. By 1090, when the Turks conquered that part of Asia Minor, scarcely any trace of the city's former glory remained. No stone of the Temple of Artemis was standing; grassy swamps covered everything; even the Christian church had disappeared into the ooze. About 1100, when the Crusaders passed through Asia Minor on their way south to liberate Jerusalem, they stopped in the muddy little Turkish village of Ayasalouk, which once had been wonderful Ephesus, and asked to see the famous Greek temple that ancient writers had praised so highly. "Temple?" the natives asked. "What temple? We have no temple here."

The Ephesians had forgotten their temple; but it remained alive in the memories of educated men, and during the nineteenth century, that first great era of archaeology, the initial attempt was made to discover its ruins. In 1863 the British Museum sent John Turtle Wood, a British architect, to search for the temple.

Wood was an energetic and high-spirited man, who relished the strange beauty of the desolate place and felt an almost mystical need to discover and excavate the

Temple of Artemis. But he met with constant difficulties. He could not find enough workmen to do the digging; the museum had given him little money to pay those men he did find; the whole region was infested with bandits; and, worst of all, there was no sign at all of the site of the temple.

He studied the ancient writers, looking for clues. Pliny had said the temple was on marshy ground, but that was not of much help, since all of Ephesus seemed to be one vast swamp. From other Greek and Roman authorities Wood drew the information that the temple must have been close to the old city walls, and traces of those walls still remained. When he dug near them, though, he found nothing of value. After five months, he had a fair idea of where the temple was *not* located, but no hint of more positive information.

His Turkish workmen went on strike and had to be coaxed back to the digs. Another delay came when he fell from his horse and broke his collarbone. Still, by the end of 1863 Wood had opened some 75 trial pits and had cut trenches into many mounds containing ruins. He had found an assortment of Greek, Roman, and early Christian buildings, but not the Temple of Artemis. (His archaeological methods left something to be desired, at times. Once he used gunpowder to blow up an early Christian church that was keeping him from getting at an older structure.)

In 1864 the story was the same. His employers, the British Museum, grew impatient at the lack of results, but Wood sent home enough crates of sculpture from other Ephesian buildings to satisfy the museum officials, and they renewed his grant. The Temple of Artemis remained undiscovered, somewhere in the swamp. In 1865, while paying a call at the British Consulate in the Turkish town of Smyrna, fifty miles from Ephesus, Wood was stabbed by a madman who meant to assassinate the consul; the wound was within an inch of his heart, but in five weeks he was back at Ephesus, digging once more. He uncovered tombs, coffins, the ancient city gates, the theater, the gymnasium. Year after year, though, the temple eluded him, until it must have seemed to him that the fabled building was only a myth.

In 1868 Wood came upon a wide road made of huge limestone and marble blocks, deeply cut by chariot wheels. He suspected that this might have been the highway leading from the city to the temple; and when he found Roman tombs alongside the road, he was even more confident. Patiently he followed the road for five hundred yards. His money ran out, and he had to halt work until the British Museum agreed to finance another year's work. By then, the local farmers had planted their crops above the site of the highway, and Wood was forced to wait until after the harvest. When he dug again, farther along the ancient highway, he excavated a large stone wall, which he thought might be the outer wall of the temple precinct. He dug there in 1869, after talking the museum into letting him have funds for one more year of work, "in consideration of my having worked at this apparently hopeless enterprise for so many years." But the museum made it clear that this was the last time it would extend the grant, unless something spectacular turned up.

Knowing this was his final chance, Wood chose his spot with great care, turning at an angle from his trench to continue along the line of the wall. Almost at once he found two large stones bearing inscriptions in Latin and Greek, declaring that the wall had been built by the Emperor Augustus in the Roman equivalent of 6 B.C. The Roman historian Tacitus, Wood knew, had mentioned the construction of this wall by Augustus—close by the Temple of Artemis. So the end of the six-year quest had to be at hand. But although Wood traced the wall for 1000 feet to the north and 500 feet to the east, he was unable to find the temple before his money again ran out in the middle of the year.

Encouraged by the discovery of the inscription, the museum permitted him to go on. He resumed work at Ephesus in the fall of 1869. Though bothered by heavy rains, plagues of scorpions and snakes, and other troubles, Wood had his workmen dig pits in various places along the wall, hoping that as they cut down through the mud and water of the swamp they would at some point strike the great marble foundation of the vanished temple. On the last day of the year, more than twenty feet down in one of the holes, a workman struck his spade against stone. Wood plunged into the excavation, and saw that the Temple of Artemis had finally been found.

The strain and excitement of the work nearly broke his health; but he ignored fever and chill, and ordered the entire swampy field to be cleared of earth. It took five more years to do it. Some 132,000 cubic yards of muck had to be carted away, and in the end he had a hole in the ground 25 feet deep, 300 feet wide, and 500 feet long, in which lay all that remained of the fourth of the Seven Wonders of the Ancient World.

The most impressive find was a series of sculptured columns, in double rows at each end of the temple. Fifteen men spent fifteen days hoisting just one of these from the pit. The columns were hauled to the coast and loaded aboard a British ship; when they reached London, a team of twenty strong horses was needed to carry them to the British Museum, where they are now on display. Wood also sent chunks of painted stone to England, fragments that only hinted at the bright colors and glowing decorations of the temple in its days of greatness.

He was aware that he was excavating two temples at once. He knew that most of the ruin he saw belonged to the final temple that had been begun about 350 B.C. But he could see beneath the pavement of that temple the foundation platform of the next oldest one, that built by Croesus two hundred years earlier and destroyed by Herostratus in 356 B.C. Some parts of that temple must have been used in the one that replaced it, for among the columns found by Wood was one inscribed, "Dedicated by Croesus."

Wood had neither the time nor the funds nor the equipment to carry his excavation deeper into the marshy soil, and so he made no attempt to get down to the older levels. That task was left for another British Museum expedition in 1904–5, under the leadership of D.G. Hogarth.

Hogarth was not faced with the problem Wood had had, of finding the temple in the first place, but his work was far from simple. In the thirty years since the end of Wood's explorations, the swamp had reclaimed the temple: the excavation pit had filled with muck and was overgrown by a thick jungle of reeds ten feet high. It had to be cleared all over again. Then, as Hogarth dug past the point where Wood had stopped, he cut into underground springs, and the site began to flood. Hogarth set up a steam pump; each morning the pit had to be pumped dry, and in the afternoons the archaeologists worked, thigh-deep in slimy mud, while the site slowly filled with water again.

Despite the difficulties of such labor, Hogarth went down so far that he was able to identify five separate temples, one above the next. Temple E, the fifth from the bottom, had been the one regarded as one of the Seven Wonders of the Ancient World. Temple D, the fourth from the bottom, was the temple built by Croesus. Beneath it was Temple C, one-fourth its size—the temple designed by Chersiphron—and Temples B and A marked still older phases of the Ephesian cult of Artemis. Even these were not the oldest of all, since Ephesus had existed for at least three hundred years when Temple A was erected. But no hint at all of the earliest temples could be found, probably because they had been made of wood; nor could Wood or Hogarth discover any trace of the great statue of Artemis which, according to Pliny, had occupied the place of honor in all the successive temples at Ephesus. Only part of the stone platform on which the statue had stood, and a fragment of the goddess' altar, were unearthed.

In and around this altar Hogarth found offerings that had been brought to the goddess: crude coins made of a gold and silver alloy, earrings, bits of ivory, figurines of animals and women, amber beads, and other small objects. None of the statuettes or jewelry was in traditional Greek style; rather, their design was more typical of Asia, underscoring the oriental origin of the cult of Artemis.

When he had finished his work, Hogarth filled the excavation in, as archaeologists often do at the end of a dig. Today, a grove of trees in a marshy plain marks the site of the temple in defense of whose goddess the angry silversmiths of St. Paul's time cried out, "Great is Diana of the Ephesians!"

# 5. The Mausoleum of Halicarnassus

Halicarnassus was another of the Greek cities on the coast of Asia Minor, less than 60 miles south of Ephesus. It was settled about 900 B.C. by Greeks who migrated from the town of Troezen, in the Peloponnesus. They found this part of southwestern Asia Minor occupied by simple herdsmen called the Carians, who did not resist when the men of Troezen landed on their shore and began to build a town. Some of the Carians stayed in their hilltop pastures, tending their flocks as their ancestors had done; others went down to the coast, mingled with the newcomers, learned the Greek language and the Greek customs, and were absorbed into Halicarnassus.

Thus the new city had a mixed population. Founded and dominated by Greeks, it also had many native Carians in its makeup. The mountains of Asia Minor rose to the east, cutting off the city from the alien and barbaric people who lived inland. In its way of life, therefore, Halicarnassus looked westward toward the Greek mainland.

Life was good in Halicarnassus. The climate was excellent for growing olives and cultivating grapes. The lovely Aegean Sea lay before the city, which had an outstanding harbor, large and well sheltered. Though the city was never as large as Ephesus, it was always prosperous.

In the middle of the sixth century B.C., Croesus of Lydia conquered Halicarnassus along with the rest of Greek Asia Minor; but after a rule of little more than a decade, he was defeated by Cyrus of Persia. Persian governors now ruled such cities as Halicarnassus, but they remained Greek in spirit despite the conquest. When one of the Greek cities revolted against the Persians in 499 B.C., the others, including Halicarnassus, joined the uprising. The Persians quelled the revolt within five years and tightened their control over the Greek cities; only when the Persians carried their war to the Greek mainland did they meet defeat, with the final victory of the Greeks coming in 479

B.C. The Persians pulled back into Asia; Greece was left in peace for half a century, entering the golden age that eventually was shattered by war between Athens and Sparta.

This period—the middle of the fifth century B.C. —was the time when Herodotus of Halicarnassus lived, traveled, and wrote. He was a typical man of his city: though born in Asia Minor in a city that owed allegiance to Persia, he was Greek in every respect.

So too was Mausolus of Caria, who ruled over Halicarnassus and the surrounding territories in the century after Herodotus' time. Mausolus, a warlike and ambitious man, was descended from the shepherd folk of the Carian hills; but he spoke Greek, behaved like a Greek, and wished his simple, rugged people to follow Greek ways. His father, Hecatomnus of Mylasa, was a mountaineer chieftain who served as the local *satrap,* or governor, on behalf of the Persians. In theory Hecatomnus was supposed to take orders from the Persians; actually he was, like most other satraps, an independent prince who did as he pleased while acknowledging the Persian king as his master.

Hecatomnus put together a small kingdom covering most of Caria and some of the adjoining districts. Mausolus, when he succeeded his father as satrap in 377 B.C., extended his control over most of southwestern Asia Minor. Shrewdly, he saw that the Greek way of life had much to offer, so he forced his people to come out of their little mountain towns and live like Greeks, along the coast. Mausolus founded new cities of Greek design there and encouraged the growth of Greek democratic ideas in these cities. He even built a chain of forts in the mountains to block the Carians from going back to their old sheepherding habits.

Much of Mausolus' energy went into the development of his capital city, Halicarnassus. There he erected a large brick and marble palace for himself and his queen, Artemisia, whose name was derived from that of the goddess revered along that coast. A shrine of Apollo, a handsome waterfront boulevard, and a mighty wall were among Mausolus' other gifts to his city. But the finest of all the new buildings was the one that Queen Artemisia caused to be constructed as the tomb and monument of her husband after Mausolus' death in 353 B.C.

Queen Artemisia had been not only Mausolus' wife but also his sister, for it was the custom in Caria for the rulers to marry their own sisters. Her grief for the dead king was intense; and she resolved to honor him by giving him the most splendid tomb the world had ever seen.

And so she sent messengers to Greece, seeking the most gifted artists of the age: architects, sculptors, bronze-workers, painters, craftsmen of every sort. She said that she did not care about the expense; she demanded the best work and the best workmen, and it was a challenge that few artists could resist. The sculptor Scopas, who had guided the rebuilding of the Temple of Artemis at Ephesus just a year or so earlier, left that job to come to Halicarnassus. So did other sculptors whose fame was nearly as great: Timotheus, Bryaxis, and Leochares. The architects Satyros and Pythias accepted Artemisia's commission; and hundreds of minor craftsmen sailed across the Aegean also to take part in the construction of Mausolus' tomb.

The site chosen was a hilltop overlooking the city, where the tomb would be visible from all Halicarnassus. But no effort was made to outdo the pyramids of Egypt in massiveness. Artemisia was quite willing to let the pyramids remain the biggest tombs in the world; she would be satisfied if Mausolus' tomb was distinguished for its beauty, richness, and grace.

While the work proceeded, Artemisia carried out a maneuver worthy of her warlike husband. Mausolus had conquered the island of Rhodes, which lies in the Aegean Sea between Greece and Asia Minor, and had placed it under

Carian rule. When he died, the Rhodians rebelled at the idea of being ruled by Artemisia, who took his place on the Carian throne. They cast off their allegiance and sent a fleet to Halicarnassus to capture the Carian capital.

The Rhodian ships entered the harbor, met no resistance, and dropped anchor. Troops went ashore to take the city. Artemisia, meanwhile, lay concealed with her fleet at a secret fort that Mausolus had built in an inconspicuous place at the east end of the harbor. Quietly she led her ships through a side canal and into the main harbor, where the Carians easily seized the surprised Rhodian fleet and towed the invading ships out to sea, leaving the Rhodians stranded in Halicarnassus.

Artemisia put her own troops aboard the Rhodian ships and sailed them back to Rhodes, where, thinking their fleet was returning in victory, the citizens welcomed them into the harbor. When the ships produced Carian soldiers, Rhodes surrendered in astonishment and returned its allegiance to Halicarnassus. Artemisia built a victory monument in Rhodes. Since it was dedicated to the gods, it could not be torn down later when the Rhodians regained their independence, so they built a high wall around it to hide it.

In 351 B.C., only two years after the death of Mausolus, Artemisia herself died. The tomb of Mausolus was still incomplete, but, according to Pliny, the sculptors chose to remain and finish their work, "considering that it was at once a memorial of their own fame and of the sculptor's art." So the project was finished, now a monument to Artemisia as well as to Mausolus. It was called the Mausoleum, to honor the late king; and the word has passed into our language, for we call any large, stately tomb a mausoleum.

Nothing remains of the original Mausoleum but fragments. From these, and from the descriptions of ancient writers, we have a fairly good idea of how the building looked, although some of the details are uncertain.

The Mausoleum was set off from the surrounding city by a wall enclosing a large rectangular courtyard. In the center of this was a stone platform, which one reached by ascending a flight of marble steps. Sculptured lions guarded the sides of this staircase; the platform above was rimmed by a second wall, on which were standing figures of gods and goddesses, with statues of warriors on prancing horses at each corner.

The tomb itself stood on this platform. There was a square marble base, comprising the room in which the bodies of Mausolus and Artemisia lay; this base was decorated with sculptured reliefs on all four sides. Above it, marble columns rose, nine to a side, thirty-six in all, supporting the upper part of the structure, which was in the form of a pyramid. The pyramid was not the smooth-sided kind favored in Egypt, but was made up of twenty-four steps, tapering toward the summit. At the flat-topped crest of the pyramid was an immense statuary group: a marble chariot, drawn by four colossal marble horses, and having as passengers the standing figures of Mausolus and Artemisia. The chariot and figures were about 25 feet high, bringing the total height of the Mausoleum to about 140 feet.

The effect was stunning and majestic. The mass of white marble, the backdrop of cypresses and olive trees, the upward rush of the structure from base to columns to pyramid to chariot, must have dazzled the onlooker's eye. The glistening stone was painted in Greek fashion: flesh-colored red, draperies tinted green, gold, or blue. The harness of the horses was done in bronze, as were the weapons of the warriors. The sculptures carved on the walls of the lower part of the Mausoleum enhanced the sense of restless, energetic movement. Here the Centaurs fought the Lapiths once again; there, Greek soldiers were locked in combat with the Amazons, a race of warrior women; beyond, a chariot race was depicted in all its tension and conflict. Figures lunged or drew back, locked together in the rhythms of battle, alternately straining and relaxing. And the marble king and queen looked down on their city.

Across the centuries Mausolus and Artemisia continued to survey Halicarnassus from on high, while tourists reverently gazed at this Wonder of the World, and while Halicarnassus itself went through many shifts of fortune. In 334 B.C. there came to it Alexander the Great, marching through Asia Minor on his campaign to conquer Persia. Alexander had previously done what no man before him had ever managed to do: he had welded the scores of stubbornly independent Greek city-states into one nation. He was not really a Greek himself, but rather a Macedonian, a man from the rough, mountainous country north of Greece proper. The Greeks regarded Macedonians as barbarians; the Macedonians envied and admired Greek culture, while scorning the weakness and small size of the individual Greek city-states.

The Greeks were unable to halt young Alexander and his fierce Macedonian legions; and after subduing Greece, the twenty-two-year-old prince crossed into Asia with 40,000 men, determined to conquer Persia and all the rest of the world. At Halicarnassus his ambitions nearly were checked. Memnon of Rhodes, the Persian commander-in-chief, led the defense; the Persians were aided by Greek troops, who together were able to hold off the Macedonians for many weeks. When Alexander succeeded in breaking through the eastern wall of the city, the Halicarnassians foiled him by hastily putting up an inner wall of brick. Then, violating the usual tactics of the besieged, the defenders came out and went on the offensive, nearly defeating Alexander; only the strength of Macedonian reinforcements saved him. In this battle, though, Halicarnassus had lost a great deal of strength, and its citizens were forced to abandon the city to the invaders. When the Macedonians finally broke into Halicarnassus they did great damage, particularly in the struggle to uproot a Persian garrison that had refused to flee. But the Mausoleum remained unharmed through all the savage fighting.

A century later, Halicarnassus passed into the control of Egypt; then it once more became an independent city. It survived heavy attacks by pirates between 62 and 58 B.C. Eventually it converted to Christianity. In medieval times it acquired a population of Turkish Moslems, who called it Bodrum, the name it bears today.

In the thirteenth and fourteenth centuries A.D. the Crusaders, when they were driven out of Palestine by the Turks, began to settle on the coast of Asia Minor and on such neighboring islands as Rhodes and Cyprus. In time they came to Bodrum, where they built an immense fortified castle in about A.D. 1400.

By this time, the Mausoleum was some seventeen centuries old, and for all those years, it seems, the final sleep of Mausolus and Artemisia had been undisturbed. The pagan monument to an all-but-forgotten ruler of a vanished era still glistened in something close to its original beauty above Halicarnassus. All about it lay the ruins of Mausolus' once-mighty city; and the Crusaders, as was their custom, used the tumbled blocks of these buildings to construct their own walls and fortresses.

At the beginning of the fifteenth century a series of earthquakes shattered the columns of the Mausoleum and sent the chariot and its riders crashing down. By A.D. 1404 only the square base of the monument was still intact. The Crusaders hauled most of the fallen upper part away as building stone. The stump was allowed to remain for another century and a quarter.

Then, in 1522, the Turks gathered strength for a new military effort that would sweep the last of the Crusaders out of their part of the world. More than two centuries had passed since the Crusaders had been forced out of the Holy Land, but they still held bases in a few well-protected places at the eastern end of the Mediterranean. Halicarnassus, or Bodrum, was occupied by the knightly order that had held it since the late fourteenth century, the Knights of St. John of Jerusalem.

Hearing of the Turkish invasion plans, the Grand Master of the Knights of St. John ordered that the castle be strengthened and made ready to withstand siege. What was left of the Mausoleum was broken up at this time, and its marble blocks ground to powder to provide lime for plastering. During this somber work of demolition, the Crusaders entered the base of the monument and found a passageway leading to the cellarlike burial place of Mausolus and Artemisia. By candlelight they made their way into a handsome square chamber, its walls adorned by beautiful sculptures, which they admired briefly and marked for destruction by the lime-makers. They could see, beyond this chamber, a second room that contained a great coffin. But they did not enter that room, for it was growing late, and they decided to return in the morning. When they came back the next day, they found that other intruders had visited the tomb in the night. The coffin was open; some fragments of cloth-of-gold were lying about, but nothing else, and the bodies of Mausolus and his queen were gone. The Knights of St. John insisted that the grave-robbers must have been Moslem villagers; but very likely some of the Crusaders themselves had plundered the grave of the ancient monarchs, stealing the treasure that had gone undisturbed for eighteen hundred years, and destroying the bodies of the Carian rulers.

Even the Crusaders could not bring themselves to turn all the noble sculpture of the Mausoleum into lime. They removed some of the best pieces and mounted them in the walls of their castle. Soon after, the Turks burst into Bodrum and the Knights of St. John fled; Bodrum Castle, with its fragments of the Mausoleum still in place, passed into Turkish hands.

Over the next three centuries many visitors came to admire these sculptures, which were recognized to be remnants of one of the Seven Wonders of the Ancient World. In the nineteenth century, when the British Museum launched its program of collecting the finest relics of antiquity, it acquired some of them. This was done simply by having the British Ambassador to Turkey ask the Turkish Sultan, in 1846, if he might remove certain pieces from Bodrum Castle and ship them to London. The Sultan, who had little interest in antiquity, granted permission.

In 1856 the British Museum sent an archaeologist, Charles Thomas Newton, to search for other surviving pieces of the Mausoleum. The walls of Bodrum Castle still contained some of the stone lions that once had flanked the main staircase of the Mausoleum, and Newton was able to obtain several of these. Then he turned to the site where the Mausoleum itself had been, and found the ground littered with sculpture that the Crusaders had not bothered to destroy. In 1857 he began to excavate.

Newton was faced at once with a problem encountered by many archaeologists in the Near East. He knew the approximate location of the Mausoleum, but not its exact position on the hill where he had found the fragments. The hill was cut into a patchwork of tiny properties, each owned by a Turkish peasant who demanded huge sums for his land. Newton could not afford to buy the whole district, so he had to proceed with care and great shrewdness.

First he consulted Pliny and other ancient authorities who mentioned the Mausoleum, and from their writings was able to calculate the approximate size and position of the monument. Then he obtained one plot of land, dug down, and drove a tunnel through the site. He found a wall, a pavement, a staircase, and a ten-ton block of green stone, which probably had been used to close the tomb. This underground probing enabled Newton to locate three of the four corners of the Mausoleum's foundation; now he knew which plots of land he needed to buy.

In the excavation that followed, Newton found four slabs of the sculptured reliefs of Greeks and Amazons, supposedly the work of the great Scopas, and many other bits of the Mausoleum's decorations. He discovered pieces of the steps making up the pyramid that had surmounted the monument; from these, he learned that the architect had attempted to create the optical illusion that the massive pyramid rested on the slim marble columns, when actually it was supported by the central chamber of the temple behind the columns. (He could tell this from the way the steps were hollowed out and grooved to fit into one another.) Newton also found a fragment of a huge chariot wheel, seven feet seven inches in diameter, which was part of the sculpture crowning the pyramid; and, most exciting of all, he uncovered the statues of Mausolus and Artemisia themselves, the riders in the chariot.

These sad reminders of vanished glories now are assembled in a special room of the British Museum—the Mausoleum Room. Here the broken chariot wheel can be seen; here are displayed the battered, weatherworn reliefs of Centaurs and Lapiths, Greeks and Amazons, defiant enemies frozen forever in a moment of fierce action; here stands the ten-foot image of Mausolus, a handsome, bearded man whose features are at once strong and calm; and beside him is his wife and sister, Artemisia, who built for him one of the most beautiful of all tombs. In the same room stands a large model of the Mausoleum, showing it as the museum experts think it must have looked, and serving as a reminder that all earthy things in time pass away.

# 6. The Colossus of Rhodes

About fifty years after the death of Mausolus, work began on the next of the Seven Wonders: a gigantic statue of Helios, the Greek sun-god, whom the people of the isle of Rhodes regarded as their special protector. Rhodes had recently been saved from invaders, and out of gratitude, the Rhodians erected this mighty statue, the Colossus of Rhodes. Of all the Wonders it was the shortest-lived, standing only fifty-six years, but in that brief time it won fame throughout the entire civilized world.

*Colossus* is actually a Latin word; the Romans borrowed it from the Greeks, who spelled it *colossos*. It meant any statue that was much larger than life size; Herodotus speaks of the *colossoi* of Egypt, such as the Sphinx and certain statues of the Pharaohs. The statues of Zeus and Athena produced by Phidias for Olympia and the Parthenon were also regarded as *colossoi*, as were other statues of the gods found in Greece. But the great Rhodian statue eclipsed all others; after that, there might be many *colossoi*, but there was only one Colossus, that of Rhodes.

Rhodes is an island off the southwestern tip of Asia Minor, where the Aegean Sea meets the Mediterranean. Its strategic location on an important sea route made it important from the earliest days of naval commerce in the eastern Mediterranean. Ships bound for Crete and the Greek mainland from Egypt or Phoenicia would call there; and Rhodian seafarers ranged the whole region as far west as Italy, bringing great wealth to their small island home. By the time Athens came to dominate the Greek world in the fifth century B.C., Rhodes already had a thousand years of greatness behind it.

During most of that century Rhodes was under Athenian control; but in 412B.C., during the war between Athens and Sparta, Rhodes revolted, and became the headquarters for the fleet of Sparta and her allies. Four years later, the Rhodians laid out a new city at the best natural harbor on their island, on the northern tip. This city—also called Rhodes—was planned according to scientific principles, and its efficient design helped it to capture almost at once a great deal of commerce from other ports in the Aegean Sea.

Struggles among the Rhodians left the island helpless over the next few generations; Athens and Sparta took turns ruling it between 412 and 357 B.C., and then it was conquered by Mausolus of Halicarnassus. We have already seen how Rhodes attempted to defeat Halicarnassus after Mausolus' death, and how that plan was frustrated by the cleverness of Queen Artemisia. About 340 B.C. Rhodes passed into Persian rule, and in 332 it was captured by Alexander the Great.

The Macedonian conqueror fell ill of a fever in June, 323, and died, not quite thirty-three years old, after having built an empire that stretched from Europe to the frontiers of India. Upon his death many segments of this vast empire expelled their Macedonian garrisons and proclaimed their independence; among them was Rhodes. The rest of the empire split into several huge pieces.

Alexander had left no heir. He had taken two wives, both Asian princesses: Roxana of Bactria, and Barsine, the daughter of Darius III, last king of Persia, whom he had overthrown. Soon after Alexander's death, Roxana, who was pregnant, murdered her rival Barsine. But Alexander's only son, whom his father did not live to see, never ruled the Macedonian Empire; he and his mother were put to death in 312 B.C., to get them out of the way of the ambitious generals who claimed the throne.

These generals were known as the *diadochoi,* or "successors." In Alexander's lifetime they had served at his side, helping him win his great empire; once he was gone they murdered all of his surviving relatives, and fought bitterly among themselves for power. In the end three of them, Ptolemy, Seleucus, and Antigonus, emerged triumphant;

unable to defeat each other, they agreed on dividing most of Alexander's territory. Ptolemy took Egypt; Seleucus took western Asia, including Persia; Antigonus took Macedon and the rest of Alexander's European possessions.

In the long and fierce struggle among these men, Rhodes chose to support Ptolemy of Egypt. It was a shrewd commercial move, for Rhodes saw profitable business in serving as the middleman between the revived land of Egypt and the markets of Greece. Alexandria, the bustling new capital of Egypt under Ptolemy, was just across the Mediterranean from Rhodes.

But the ties between Ptolemy and the Rhodians angered grim, one-eyed old King Antigonus of Macedon. In 307 B.C. he sent his son, Demetrius, to punish Rhodes for having assisted Ptolemy in the wars of the *diadochoi*.

Demetrius brought an army of 40,000 men—more than the entire population of Rhodes—and bolstered his forces by collecting some bands of Aegean pirates. Demetrius also included a special corps of engineers in his army, for Rhodes presented a real challenge: it was guarded by a strong, high wall. In the warfare of that time, such a wall could be broken only by powerful catapults hurling heavy stone balls, or scaled by soldiers using siege towers that could be rolled up to the wall. Demetrius called on his engineers to provide him with the greatest assortment of military machinery that his era had ever seen.

The attackers moved in from sea, under cover of darkness. For this stage of the invasion Demetrius relied heavily on four floating siege engines, each made up of two ships lashed together, and carrying four-story towers equipped with catapults. Making a surprise attack, Demetrius was able to capture the mole, or stone breakwater, protecting the harbor of Rhodes. He stationed his siege engines here, using them to set up a bombardment of the city that would cover the attack of his troops. While the catapults flung 180-pound balls into Rhodes, landing craft carried Demetrius' troops to shore.

The outnumbered Rhodians fought back desperately. They drove off the invading soldiers, and sank two of Demetrius' floating siege engines with their own ships. Demetrius ordered his engineers to assemble a supertower mounted atop six ships lashed together; but as this machine was being towed into position a storm came up and overturned it. During the confusion of the storm the Rhodians were able to recapture the mole.

Demetrius next tried to attack the city by land. Protected by eight "tortoises," or wheeled sheds, his men approached the wall of Rhodes and filled in the deep ditch that surrounded it. Then the attackers moved two gigantic ram tortoises against the wall. Each of these was a covered wheeled shed containing a battering ram 180 feet long, operated by a thousand men.

While the two rams hammered at the wall, and the smaller siege engines plagued the Rhodians by catapulting stone balls over it, Demetrius brought his mightiest war machine into action. This was a tower nearly 150 feet high, from 50 to 75 feet square at the base, and mounted on eight tremendous iron wheels. It took thirty-four hundred of Demetrius' soldiers to push this monster to the walls. Each of its nine stories was equipped with heavy artillery in the form of catapults, protected by leather shutters stuffed with wool; the shutters were raised to allow the catapult to hurl a ball into the city, then quickly lowered to shield the gunners while they readied the next shot. Each story also had a water tank for putting out fires; two sets of ladders in the tower carried traffic up and down.

Though dismayed by the sight of the huge siege tower, the Rhodians did not waver in the defense of their city. Where the battering rams of the Macedonians smashed holes in the wall, the Rhodians concentrated their strength to keep the enemy troops from breaking through, and tore down buildings to have stone for repairing the wall. Where the giant tower threatened them, they massed all their artillery for a counterattack, for they had catapults too. In a sudden night bombardment they hurled flaming missiles at the tower and set it afire.

Demetrius was forced to pull his tower and the rest of his siege engines back from the wall, so they could be repaired out of the range of the Rhodian catapults. He kept the city under siege, though, hoping to starve the Rhodians into surrender. But neither famine nor disease weakened the defenders. The little island stood fast. Women gave their hair to be made into bowstrings; slaves were armed, and promised their freedom if Demetrius were defeated.

Now Demetrius returned to the attack, bringing his rebuilt siege tower closer to the city. The Rhodians stopped it by flooding the ditch outside their wall, turning the ground into a swamp in which the 180-ton tower became hopelessly mired. Unable to use the most powerful of his war machines, Demetrius was stymied, and his army remained camped outside the walls of Rhodes for months, unable to enter the valiant city. Meanwhile, as Rhodes continued to hold out, word of the year-long siege reached Ptolemy of Egypt. Ptolemy dispatched a fleet to assist the Rhodians, and Demetrius was forced to lift the siege and withdraw when the Egyptian ships arrived. He left his engines of war behind as he made his hasty retreat. The grateful Rhodians gave Ptolemy the nickname of *Soter*, "savior," and sarcastically tagged Demetrius with the name of *Polyorketes*, "besieger of cities."

To show their thankfulness for being delivered from their attackers, the Rhodians resolved to build a colossal statue—not of Ptolemy Soter, for that would have been blasphemous, but rather of Helios, the sun-god, whom they looked upon as their special deity. They smashed up some of the abandoned war machines of Demetrius Polyorketes, melting the metal parts to get bronze for the statue, and sold some of the other engines to pay the cost of the work. The giant siege tower was used as the scaffolding for the construction of the Colossus.

Chares of Lindos, a Rhodian sculptor who had fought in the defense of the city, was chosen to design and construct the statue. He had been the pupil of Lysippus, the favorite sculptor of Alexander the Great, who had produced several colossi of his own, including a 60-foot statue of Zeus. But Chares planned a work that would dwarf the the greatest achievement of his teacher Lysippus. He would create the largest bronze statue ever made.

Most of the stories that have come down to us concerning the Colossus of Rhodes are fantasies, made up centuries after the real facts were forgotten. We have two chief ancient sources of information about the Colossus. One is the book about the Seven Wonders that is credited to Philon of Byzantium, who lived a century after the statue had collapsed; but this book was almost certainly written several hundred years after Philon's time. The other is Pliny's *Natural History*, written three centuries after the toppling of the Colossus. Pliny, who devotes only a paragraph to the Colossus, says that it took twelve years to complete, and this is probably correct: historians believe that the Colossus was begun in 304 B.C. and finished in 292 B.C. The book of Philon says the statue cost the immense sum of 300 talents, or nearly 18,000 pounds of silver. This is about $5,000,000 in modern money, and vastly more in terms of the value of money in ancient times.

Evidently Chares died before the job was done. This inspired a number of tales, which we must look upon with suspicion. According to one version, the original plan of the Colossus called for it to be about fifty feet high. When the Rhodians decided to double the height, the story goes,

Chares asked for only twice the original fee, forgetting the mathematical rule that increasing the surface dimensions of an object produces a much greater increase in its mass and volume. Thus, doubling the planned size of the Colossus meant an *eightfold* increase in the building material required; and since Chares was supposed to pay for all material used out of his fee, this oversight drove him into bankruptcy and led him to commit suicide. So it was told by Sextus Empiricus, who lived in the second century A.D. But it seems highly unlikely that an experienced craftsman like Chares could have forgotten, even for a moment, so basic a law of the sculptor's trade. Another story claims that when the Colossus was nearly finished, someone pointed out to Chares a trifling error in the statue's construction, and he was so humiliated by the flaw that he committed suicide. But there is no proof this tale is true.

In the Middle Ages it was often said that the Colossus stood 900 feet tall. This could not have been possible, for Chares' great statue was made of bronze on an iron framework, and a structure so high, fashioned from those materials, would not have been strong enough to stand. More reliable accounts of ancient times indicate that the height of the Colossus was about 160 feet—110 feet for the statue itself, 50 feet more for the stone pedestal on which it stood. Thus the Colossus and the Statue of Liberty in New York Harbor would have been virtual twins in size, for the Statue of Liberty stands 111 feet from heel to crown, rising 40 feet more to the tip of the torch held in the uplifted arm. Lady Liberty weighs 225 tons; she consists of 100 tons of copper sheeting over steel girders. Chares did not have steel to use for his statue's framework, so it must have been more massive than the Statue of Liberty to make up for the relative weakness of its materials; its weight was probably about 300 tons. The book of Philon of Byzantium says that it contained 15 tons of bronze and

9 tons of iron, but this is certainly a great underestimation. Such a quantity would have produced bronze sheeting only one-sixteenth of an inch thick, and the first strong wind would have hurled the statue over. It is more likely that the bronze used was at least an inch thick.

The most foolish of the tales told about the Colossus asserts that the statue stood spread-legged on two different moles, straddling the harbor of Rhodes so that all ships had to sail beneath it. The origin of this wild idea lay in the existence of two ancient moles in the harbor.

If the statue really had spanned the harbor with one foot planted on each of them, it would have had to be close to half a mile high, for the moles lay 400 yards apart. Also, the port of Rhodes would have had to be shut down altogether for a dozen years while the statue was being built, and this would hardly have been done. There is no ancient account of the Colossus that says anything about so dramatic a pose, nor would a Greek sculptor have been likely to depict a god in such an awkward and undignified manner. Finally, in practical engineering terms, it could not have been possible to build a bronze and iron statue of such size with slanting legs.

We have to rely on indirect evidence for our ideas of what the Colossus did look like. The god Helios was usually depicted with a crown of spiked "rays" on his head, like that of the Statue of Liberty; this is the way he appears on Greek coins and small statues of the time, and probably the Colossus looked that way. A badly damaged sculptured relief found on Rhodes just before World War II is possibly an actual copy of the Colossus; it shows a nude figure crowned with the sun-rays of Helios, beardless, long-haired, with the right hand raised as if to shade the eyes from the light of the rising sun. A cloak is draped over the left arm.

Archaeologists are not even sure of the exact site where

the Colossus stood, but it is generally thought that it rose at the tip of the main mole. This ancient breakwater juts across the harbor in such a way that the statue could have been placed to look eastward, toward the dawning sun, so that the first beams of morning would make its bronze skin gleam with blinding brilliance. Limestone blocks lying in the sea near this mole may have been part of the inner structure of the Colossus.

The book credited to Philon of Byzantium gives a detailed description of the construction of the huge statue. First the captured siege tower of Demetrius Polyorketes was brought to the site of the Colossus to serve as a scaffold. Within this square wooden framework, two or three stone columns were erected as the main supports of the Colossus. Iron rods were driven into these columns, extending out to the surface of the statue. The statue's bronze skin was cast in the form of large plates that were riveted to each other and to the skeleton of iron rods.

Shaping these plates called for great skill. They had to be huge, for the Colossus measured about sixty feet around the chest, was eleven feet thick at the thigh, five feet at the ankle, yet each plate had to be a realistic imitation of part of a human body. It is thought that Chares made plaster models, about three feet high, for each section of the Colossus. The craftsmen shaping the plates would cast them and allow them to cool, and then, probably, compared them to the plaster models and hammered them to the exact shape desired. Only after they satisfied Chares were they mounted on the iron skeleton.

To get the plates to their proper position, Chares adopted the method that had been used some twenty-two centuries before his time in constructing the pyramids of Egypt. He built an earthen mound around the statue as it grew; the workmen simply had to carry the plates up a sloping ramp. The lower parts of the statue remained completely hidden in the mound, which toward the end of the project must have been the size of a small hill. At last the sun-god's crown went into place; the earth was shoveled off and carted away, the skin of the Colossus received its final polishing, and the scaffolding was removed.

For fifty-six years the majestic figure commanded the harbor of Rhodes. The great shining image of the god, more than twenty times the height of a man, awed all who sailed to Rhodes. The Statue of Liberty, huge as it is, seems lost in the vastness of New York Harbor, but the Colossus of Rhodes, much closer to shore in a much smaller harbor, must have been overwhelming. Then, late in the third century B.C., an earthquake threw it down. It fell in pieces along the mole, and there it lay for hundreds of years. One Egyptian ruler, it is said, offered the people of Rhodes the equivalent of millions of dollars if they would reconstruct it; but the Rhodians, possibly fearing the statue had in some way displeased Helios, rejected the offer.

"Even as it lies," Pliny wrote in the first century A.D., "it excites our wonder and admiration. Few men can clasp the thumb in their arms, and its fingers are larger than most statues. Where the limbs are broken asunder, vast caverns are seen yawning in the interior. Within it, too, are to be seen large masses of rock, by the weight of which the artist steadied it while erecting it."

Six centuries after Pliny's time, the Arabs conquered Rhodes, and held it from A.D. 653 to 658. During those years a general finished the job of destruction by having the big fragments broken up into smaller pieces and shipped to Syria to be sold as junk. There they were bought by a dealer in scrap metal, who carried the remains of the Colossus of Rhodes away on the backs on nine hundred camels. He melted down the bronze, for sale to makers of trays and lamps throughout the Near East. Of all the dooms that came to the various Wonders, this seems the most sad.

# 7. The Lighthouse of Alexandria

The roster of the Seven Wonders begins and ends in Egypt, but the Egypt in which the Lighthouse of Alexandria was built differed tremendously from the Egypt of the Great Pyramid of Khufu. An enormous span of time separates the first and last of the Seven Wonders; Khufu's Pyramid was as old, at the time of the construction of the Lighthouse, as the Lighthouse would be today if it still existed. Some twenty-three centuries divide the Pyramid from the Lighthouse, and twenty-three more centuries divide the Lighthouse from our own era.

Khufu, if he could have arisen after more than two thousand years to inspect the Egypt in which the Lighthouse was rising, would have been baffled by the changes that had come over his land. His own Pyramid was still there, of course, and he would not have been surprised to find beside it the somewhat smaller pyramids of his immediate successors. But he would have been astonished to learn that the Pharaoh was no longer regarded as a living god; that in fact there were no more Pharaohs, and Egypt now was ruled by Greeks and Macedonians, men of a land that had been unknown in Khufu's day. The old religion, too, was gone, and had been replaced several times over. Re, the sun-god whom Khufu worshipped, was forgotten; another god named Osiris had taken his place, and then a god named Amon had arisen. But now even these deities, who at least were Egyptian, were giving way to the strange gods of the Greeks—Zeus and Hera and Hermes and others—whom Egypt's conquerors had brought with them. Although the people still spoke the old language, hardly anyone understood how to use the hieroglyphic writing of Khufu's era; the Greek alphabet was what most of the merchants and scribes employed. For the peasants of Egypt, perhaps, not much had changed in those twenty-three centuries, but everything else—government, religion, culture—was tainted by the influence of the Greeks. Even the old capital, Memphis, had ceased to be the center of authority. Egypt's new masters ruled from a place far to the north, at the edge of the Mediterranean Sea. Their capital was a city named in honor of the Macedonian conqueror, Alexander the Great. And this strange city called Alexandria, Khufu would think, was the source of all the changes that had come upon his land.

Alexander, who was not a modest man, scattered cities of that name through all his sprawling empire; he founded three Alexandrias in India alone. Most of the seventeen known Alexandrias vanished long ago, but one, that of Egypt, became an enduring city, and today has a population of more than a million.

The site that Alexander chose in 332 B.C. for Egypt's Alexandria was at the western end of the Nile delta, in a region that had never been important during the reign of the Pharaohs. There already were Greek settlements in that part of northern Egypt, merchant colonies several centuries old, and Alexander could have picked one of those for his capital. But he wished to make a fresh start, creating a new city in Egypt that would be purely Greek in outlook and style.

He decided to build it in a flat, sandy wasteland occupied only by a tiny fishing village, Rhakotis. The Nile, on which all of Egypt's other major cities had been built, was twenty miles away. The site of Rhakotis was a spit of land a mile and a half wide, lying between the Mediterranean and swampy Lake Mareotis.

Putting his capital so far from Egypt's great river was a clever stroke. Alexander wanted the new city to become a major Mediterranean seaport; but he knew that wherever the Nile met the sea, the river dumped so much silt and mud into the shore area that any harbor soon would be choked. That would be no problem at Alexandria. The city would have two harbors, both of them always clear: a

Mediterranean harbor on its north side, and a freshwater harbor to the south, facing Lake Mareotis. A canal from the lake to the Nile would connect Alexandria with the river ports of southern Egypt. Thus the city would be open to the Mediterranean trade in one direction, to the Nile trade in the other, without fear of being strangled by the huge quantities of mud that the Nile carried northward.

Alexander gave to Deinocrates of Rhodes, the outstanding architect of his time, the task of planning the city. Deinocrates laid it out in an orderly way, with streets crossing at right angles and a magnificent boulevard, one hundred feet wide and lined with columns, running the length of the city from east to west. Room was left for spacious parks and gardens, for splendid palaces, a zoo, a museum, and a library. A mile-long breakwater would protect the harbor on the Mediterranean side, running from the shore to a nearby island called Pharos. Alexander dreamed of a glorious metropolis that would attract scholars, poets, scientists, merchants, mariners, all those who make a city great. He saw the marketplaces of Alexandria packed with goods from every land, and traders of many nations haggling in its shops.

This dream was far from a reality when Alexander unexpectedly died in Babylon in 323 B.C. Ptolemy Soter, who succeeded him as the ruler of Egypt, had to use the old city of Memphis as his capital while Alexandria was being completed. It was several years before Ptolemy was able to move to Alexandria. He brought with him the body of Alexander, which was laid to rest in a mausoleum said to rival in beauty the tomb of Mausolus himself. Alexander's remains were placed in a coffin of gold, although this was replaced, a century later, by a coffin of an even more marvelous substance: glass.

Alexandria under Ptolemy Soter grew rapidly toward the splendor Alexander had predicted for it. It became a dazzling city, rich and brilliant and bold, the center of cultural life in the world of twenty-three centuries ago. It was, as New York City is today, the city where most of what was new and exciting happened. The symbol of Alexandria's prosperity was its wondrous Lighthouse, which guided toward its piers the ships that brought luxury goods from all over the world.

Ptolemy Soter decreed the building of the Lighthouse about 290 B.C., but it was still unfinished when he died in 285. His son, Ptolemy II, ruled Egypt at the time this sky-scraping landmark was completed, about 270 B.C.

The Lighthouse, last of the Seven Wonders of the Ancient World, was designed by Sostrates of Knidos. Few kings of ancient times permitted any name but their own to be carved on the great structures built during their reigns, and Ptolemy II was no exception. The story goes that he refused permission for Sostrates to inscribe his name on the Lighthouse, but that the crafty architect carved these words onto a foundation stone nonetheless:

SOSTRATES SON OF DEXIPHANES OF KNIDOS
ON BEHALF OF ALL MARINERS
TO THE SAVIOR GODS

Then he covered this dedication with a layer of plaster, on which was chiseled the expected inscription in honor of Ptolemy. Over the years the plaster peeled away; Ptolemy's name disappeared and that of Sostrates could be seen.

The site of the Lighthouse was the easternmost end of the island of Pharos, in the harbor of Alexandria. When mariners approached Alexandria after the Lighthouse was built, they looked for Pharos and its Lighthouse, and spoke of "sailing in by Pharos" until the Lighthouse acquired the island's name, and was called "the Pharos" by everyone. Many languages still keep the word. A lighthouse is *faro* in Italian and Spanish, *phare* in French. English seamen of Queen Elizabeth's time called any lighthouse a pharos, and some sailors today use the word when referring to a ship's lantern or any other bright light seen at sea.

The Pharos of Alexandria was destroyed in medieval times, but several descriptions of it have come down to us, the work of two Moslem travelers of the twelfth century: Idrisi, a Moorish geographer from Spain, who visited it about 1115, and Yusuf Ibn al-Shaikh, another Moorish scholar of Spain, who saw the Pharos about fifty years later. They measured the building, counted its stairs and galleries, and set down their impressions of how it looked. The only difficulty with the measurements they gave is that we cannot translate them easily into modern feet. They used the cubit as their unit of measurement; but the length of the cubit varied from place to place, and we do not know which cubit they had in mind. Most often the cubit was eighteen of our inches, but it had a length of nearly two feet in some regions. So when Idrisi and Yusuf tell us that the Pharos was 300 cubits in height, we cannot be sure if they mean about 450 feet or almost 600 feet.

In any case it was a colossal structure, the tallest of its era. Unlike modern lighthouses, which usually are slim, tapering towers, the Pharos looked something like a twentieth-century skyscraper, built in several setback stages. The base was a square, massive building resting on a heavy stone platform. The handsome blocks of white marble of which the platform and the Pharos were made were joined not by any ordinary mortar but by molten lead, to reinforce the building against the constant pounding of the waves. Within the square bottom section were government offices and military barracks, as well as stables for three hundred horses.

Above this section was a long, narrow, eight-sided section. There was a broad balcony where this part of the Pharos began, and here refreshments were sold to tourists climbing the tower: pieces of roast lamb on sticks, pomegranates and other fruits, cooling drinks. Elegant sculptured decorations ornamented this balcony.

At the upper end of the eight-sided part there was another balcony—a lookout point for the sightseers. This was from three hundred to four hundred feet above the sea, depending on what length is assigned to the cubit. Those who made the climb were able to see far out into the Mediterranean, or, from the other side, to look over all of Alexandria and Lake Mareotis beyond it.

The third and highest section of the Pharos was cylindrical, and led to the beacon chamber at the summit. Here a fire continually burned. Idrisi tells us, "It is kept lit night and day as a beacon for navigators throughout the whole sailing season; mariners know the fire and direct their course accordingly, for it is visible a day's sail [one hundred miles] away. By night it looks like a brilliant star; by day one can perceive its smoke."

Storytellers of the later Middle Ages, who were fond of exaggerating the marvels of ancient times, declared that the beacon chamber contained a huge mirror of "transparent stone," which greatly increased the brilliance of the light of the fire, and allowed the keepers of the Pharos to send the reflected beams as far as three hundred miles out to sea. When enemy ships approached Alexandria, they said, the mirror could be used as a magnifying glass to focus the light and set the invaders afire when they were still twenty miles away. And by looking into the mirror, one could see what was happening in the city of Constantinople, far across the sea.

Probably there is some truth at the bottom of these legends. We ought not to believe that the light of the

Pharos could reach distances of three hundred miles, or that it was able to set ships afire, or that it allowed the rulers of Alexandria to check up on doings in Constantinople. But it is altogether possible that some sort of glass mirror was employed to amplify the Pharos' beam. Still more likely, the mirror may have been made of a curved sheet of polished metal.

Within the Lighthouse a broad spiral ramp enabled horse-drawn wagons laden with fuel for the fire to be driven as far as the top of the lowest section. There, a kind of dumbwaiter arrangement allowed the fuel to be hoisted through a central shaft to the beacon chamber at the summit. Visitors ascending the Pharos also used the ramp, but staircases took them up the second and third sections. Near the top, the staircase was so narrow that one could not turn around while climbing. Hundreds of windows pierced the walls of the Pharos from top to bottom to provide light for those using the stairs and the ramp. At the very top of the Lighthouse stood a colossal statue of the sea-god Poseidon.

The Pharos was not on the original lists of the Seven Wonders of the World, which were drawn up in the century after its construction. Over the centuries, though, its astonishing height and the power of its beam won it worldwide fame, and, since Babylon was by now only a fading memory, the Pharos pushed the walls of that city from the group of Seven Wonders. Certainly the Lighthouse deserved its place on the roster. The walls of Babylon, though huge and awesome, were merely thicker versions of the walls that surrounded any important ancient city; but the Pharos, vaulting 400 feet or more into the sky, rose far above any other building of its time. (Khufu's Pyramid was 480 feet high, but that practically solid pile of stone was not the same kind of structure. Only in recent times, when steel girders came into use in construction, did buildings exceed in height the Pharos. And if it were still standing, the Lighthouse would overtop nearly all buildings of the modern world outside the United States.)

All through the years of Alexandria's greatness the Pharos blazed in the harbor. Greece itself became a minor part of the Roman Empire; but Alexandria, an outpost of Greek culture in a foreign land, was second only to the city of Rome in importance. A long line of Ptolemies presided over it. Gradually Alexandria and the rest of Egypt came under Roman control, and by 80 B.C. Alexandria formally had passed into the jurisdiction of Rome, though it still was ruled by the family of Ptolemy. Julius Caesar, who came there in 47 B.C., fell in love with Queen Cleopatra, the daughter of Ptolemy XII, and might have made her Empress of Rome if he had not been assassinated three years later. (During Caesar's stay in Alexandria the famous library, largest in the world, was destroyed by a mob rioting against Roman authority.) After Caesar's death, Cleopatra took as her lover the ambitious Mark Antony, who was trying to seize power in the empire; but Antony's schemes failed in 31 B.C., and Cleopatra committed suicide the following year lest she be taken to Rome as a prisoner. The line of the Ptolemics was broken, and Egypt became a Roman province. But the Pharos of Alexandria still stood in all its magnificence.

By the time of Christ, Alexandria's population was 300,000—not counting slaves. The city's growth continued for centuries, though it was severely crippled in A.D. 215 when the Roman Emperor Caracalla, outraged by the mockery he had received from the Alexandrians, ordered a general massacre of the citizens. Alexandria recovered, and in the following century became an important center of Christianity. But as the Roman Empire broke up, Alexandria's power began to wane. In A.D. 616 it was captured by the Persians, and thirty years later, after a siege lasting fourteen months, it was absorbed into the growing empire of the Arabs. When Cairo became the capital of Arab Egypt in the tenth century, Alexandria's decline was complete. It dwindled until at the beginning of the nineteenth century it had only 4,000 inhabitants. Prosperity did not return to it until recent times, when once again it became a leading seaport of the eastern Mediterranean.

Various stories are told of the fate of the Pharos. According to one tale, the Lighthouse remained in service for over a thousand years, but was thrown down by an earthquake in A.D. 796. Another story has it that it was partly demolished about the year 850 as a result of a bit of trickery. According to this version, the Emperor of Constantinople feared the rivalry of Alexandria as a port, and devised a clever way to fool the Arabs into depriving their own city of its Lighthouse. He sent an ambassador to the court of the Caliph at Cairo, under orders to spread rumors that a fabulous treasure was buried beneath the Pharos. These whispers eventually reached the ears of the greedy Caliph, who immediately gave word that the famed building be torn down. As the Arab workmen started to dismantle the topmost level, they let the great mirror crash to its ruin. Then they ripped away the beacon chamber and the eight-sided level below it, so that only the stump of the Lighthouse remained. Suddenly the Caliph realized that he had been fooled. He halted the demolition and tried to rebuild the tower with bricks. But it proved to be too hard a job; and in the end the Caliph had a mosque, a Moslem place of worship, built at the top of what was left of the Pharos.

It is an interesting story, but there does not seem to be much truth in it. When the Moor Idrisi visited Alexandria in A.D.1115, the entire structure was still intact, as is clear from his detailed description, including measurements of each level. Idrisi plainly stated that the Pharos was in use as a lighthouse. Yusuf Ibn al-Shaikh, touring the Pharos in 1165, also found it in good condition, although by then it had ceased to serve its original purpose. In his time a small mosque had been installed on the highest level in place of the beacon. But he was able to go to the top of the building, to take many measurements, and to inspect the mosque.

About A.D. 1375, the Pharos met the fate that had come to so many others of the Seven Wonders: it was toppled by an earthquake. The broken blocks of the mighty building fell into Alexandria's harbor, interfering with shipping; it took a hundred years to clear the channel of the biggest pieces. The stump of the tower still stood at the tip of the breakwater, and in A.D. 1480 Kait Bey, the Sultan of Egypt, built a castle and fortress there, using the remnants of the base of the Pharos for the walls of his structure.

The rest of the Pharos lies somewhere on the floor of the sea in Alexandria's harbor. No one knows where. Skin divers have explored the harbor thoroughly, and have found many items of archaeological interest—Roman coins, granite columns, coffins of marble. Occasionally something has been found that may have been a piece of the Lighthouse. This happened early in 1962, when a young Egyptian slipped into the water to spear some fish. He was only a few yards off shore, at a depth of twenty-four feet, when he saw fragments of a very large statue—one piece alone was twenty feet long. Near it, he came upon a smaller statue, a column, and a sphinx.

Dr. Henry Riad, curator of the Greco-Roman Museum at Alexandria, suggested that the huge statue might be that of Poseidon, which once had stood atop the Pharos. Egyptian naval divers were sent down, and they confirmed the original diver's report of statuary of colossal size. But the water was too rough and too muddy to permit photographing the ruins, and thus far nothing, apparently, has been done to bring them to the surface.

Alexandria has a modern lighthouse to guide ships in at night. But it is hardly more than a tenth as lofty as the Pharos, and voyagers pay little attention to it as they enter the harbor that once boasted one of the Seven Wonders of the World.

# Afterword

And so we conclude our tour of the Seven Wonders of the Ancient World. The game of listing wonders can still be played, though. Some years ago, the American Society of Civil Engineers held a contest to compile a list of Seven Wonders of the Modern World, and came up with these:

- Chicago's Sewage Disposal System
- The Colorado River Aqueduct
- Grand Coulee Dam
- Hoover Dam
- The Panama Canal
- The San Francisco-Oakland Bay Bridge
- The Empire State Building

The ancient makers of such lists, if they could see this one, would probably have objected to including two dams, on grounds of similarity, and perhaps they would have wondered a bit about the Chicago sewer system, remarkable engineering feat though that is. But surely they would have admitted one of our great bridges to any list of modern wonders, one of our skyscrapers, one of our huge dams. Other possibilities for a group of Seven Wonders of today might be the Jodrell Bank radio-telescope, which monitors the entire universe; the Cape Kennedy space center; the Lincoln Memorial, which so closely resembles a Greek temple; the Statue of Liberty; the Taj Mahal, which a grieving seventeenth-century ruler of India built as a tomb for his wife; the Cathedral of Notre Dame, in Paris, greatest example of Gothic architecture; or one of the giant power plants where electricity is produced from atomic energy. All these, and others, are worth consideration. Here, though, is my own list of Seven Wonders of the Modern World. Perhaps yours will be quite different, for we live in an age when wonders are abundant.

1. *The Empire State Building, New York.* At 1,250 feet it is still the tallest building in the world, although others now under construction will exceed it. Even so, the Empire State is likely to remain the best known of our giant buildings for a long time.
2. *The Washington Monument.* This 555-foot shaft of stone is a memorial to a great leader of the past, a symbol of our country's birth, an instantly recognizable image of the upward thrust of the United States across two centuries.
3. *Christ the Redeemer, Brazil.* This hundred-foot-tall statue of Jesus, atop a peak 2,200 feet high overlooking Rio de Janeiro, is one of the most spectacular religious monuments in the world, comparable in impact, perhaps, to the huge figure of Zeus at Olympia.
4. *Grand Coulee Dam, Washington State.* The most massive man-made structure in the world, with a volume of 10 million cubic yards of concrete, this dam is so wide that four ocean liners the size of the *Queen Elizabeth* could moor side by side in front of it.
5. *The San Francisco-Oakland Bay Bridge.* This elaborate structure spans an eight-mile gap, four and a half miles of it over water. It is made up of two 2,300-foot suspension bridges built end to end, a tunnel, and a 1,400-foot bridge of the cantilever type. Though such single-

span bridges as the Golden Gate in San Francisco and the George Washington and Verrazano Narrows Bridges in New York are longer than any one section of the Bay Bridge, the Bay Bridge is unequalled for sheer complexity and massiveness, and the unusual methods by which its construction problems were solved make it an engineering landmark.

6. *The Panama Canal.* Centuries-old patterns of seagoing commerce were transformed when this mammoth ditch was cut through Central America, linking the Atlantic and Pacific Oceans.
7. *The United Nations Building, New York.* Neither the tallest nor the most beautiful of skyscrapers, this tower of glass embodies mankind's hope that civilization will endure, that the powers of self-destruction now in human hands will never be unleashed, that there will be future generations able to look back on our own era and its many wonders.

# Bibliography

Aldred, Cyril. *The Egyptians.* London: Thames and Hudson, 1961.

Barr, Stringfellow. *The Will of Zeus: A History of Greece.* Philadelphia: Lippincott, 1961.

*Cambridge Ancient History.* Vol. 5, Athens 478–401 B.C. Cambridge: University Press, 1927.

——— Vol. 6, Macedon 401–301 B.C. Cambridge: University Press, 1927.

Ceram, C. W. *Gods, Graves, and Scholars.* New York: Alfred A. Knopf, 1951.

Champdor, Albert. *Babylon.* New York: Putnam, 1958.

Cook, J. M. *The Greeks in Ionia and the East.* London: Thames and Hudson, 1961.

Cook, R. M. *The Greeks Till Alexander.* London: Thames and Hudson, 1961.

Cottrell, Leonard. *Wonders of Antiquity.* London: Longmans Green, 1960.

De Camp, L. Sprague. *The Ancient Engineers.* New York: Doubleday, 1962.

Edwards, I. E. S. *The Pyramids of Egypt.* Harmondsworth, England: Penguin Books, 1961.

Fairservis, Walter A. *Egypt, Gift of the Nile.* New York: The Macmillan Company, 1963.

Graves, Robert. *The Greek Myths.* New York: George Braziller, 1957.

Herodotus, *The History.* Many editions in print.

Koldewey, Robert. *The Excavations at Babylon.* London: Macmillan and Co., 1914.

MacKendrick, Paul. *The Greek Stones Speak.* New York: St. Martin's Press, 1962.

Mertz, Barbara. *Temples, Tombs, and Hieroglyphs.* New York: Coward-McCann, 1964.

Parrot, Andre. *Babylon and the Old Testament.* New York: Philosophical Library, 1968.

Pliny. *Natural History.* 6 vols. London: Bohn Classical Library, 1855.

Sarton, George. *A History of Science.* 2 vols. Cambridge: Harvard University Press, 1952, 1959.

Silverberg, Robert. *Empires in the Dust.* Philadelphia: Chilton, 1963.

——— *Lost Cities and Vanished Civilizations.* Philadelphia: Chilton, 1962.

# Index

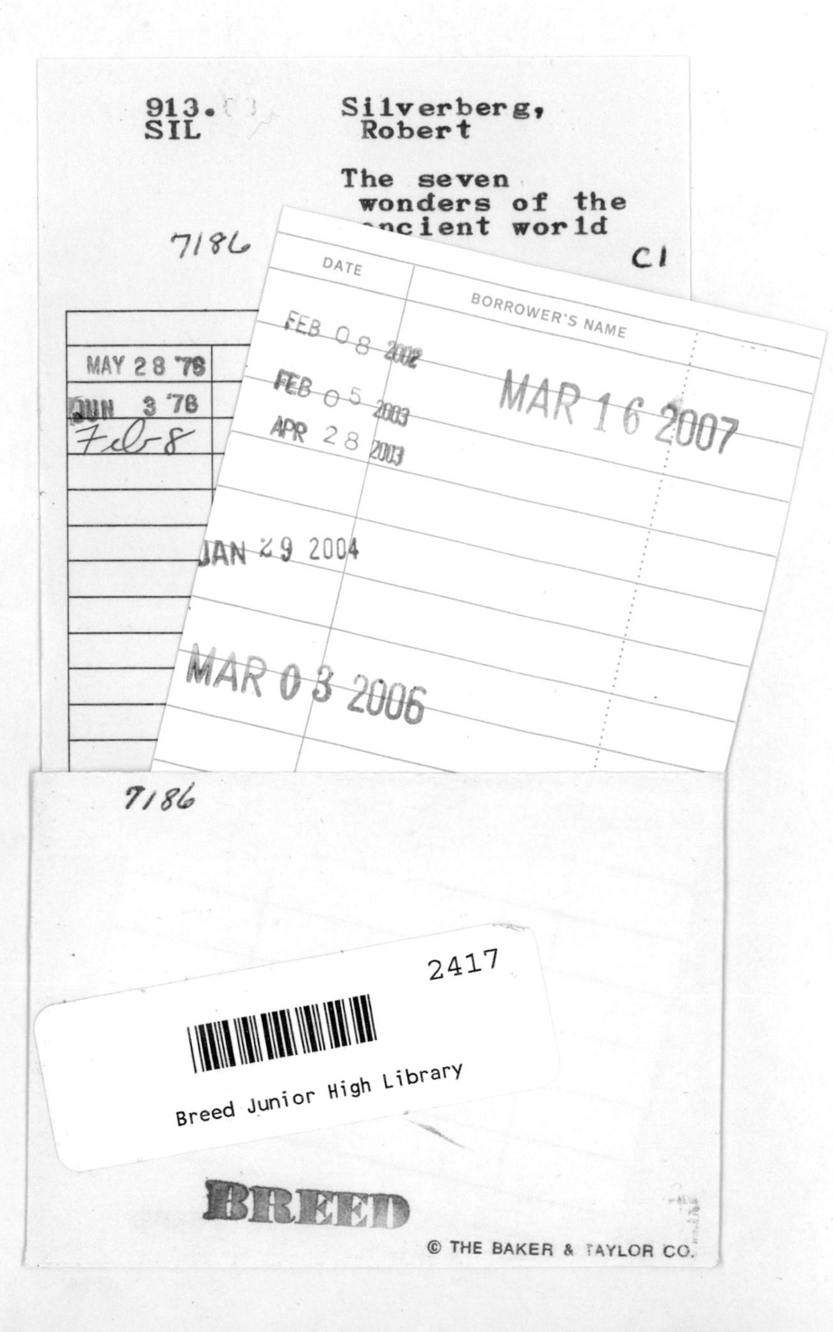
913.
SIL
Silverberg,
Robert
The seven
wonders of the
ancient world
7186
C1
MAY 28 '76
JUN 3 '76
Feb 8
DATE
BORROWER'S NAME
FEB 08 2002
MAR 16 2007
FEB 05 2003
APR 28 2003
JAN 29 2004
MAR 03 2006
7186
2417
Breed Junior High Library
BREED
© THE BAKER & TAYLOR CO.